Coordinating the curriculum in the smaller primary school

THE SUBJECT LEADER'S HANDBOOKS

Series Editor: Mike Harrison, Centre for Primary Education,
School of Education, The University of Manchester,
Oxford Road, Manchester, M13 9DP

Coordinating mathematics across the primary school
Tony Brown

Coordinating English at Key Stage 1
Jenny Tyrrell

Coordinating English at Key Stage 2
Mick Waters and Tony Martin

Coordinating science across the primary school
Lynn D. Newton and Douglas P. Newton

Coordinating information and communications technology across the
primary school
Mike Harrison

Coordinating art across the primary school
Robert Clements, Judith Piotrowski and Ivy Roberts

Coordinating design and technology across the primary school
Alan Cross

Coordinating geography across the primary school
John Halocha

Coordinating history across the primary school
Julie Davies and Jason Redmond

Coordinating music across the primary school
Sarah Hennessy

Coordinating religious education across the primary school
Derek Bastide

Coordinating physical education across the primary school
Carole Raymond

Management skills for SEN coordinators
Sylvia Phillips, Jennifer Goodwin and Rosita Heron

Building a whole school assessment policy
Mike Wintle and Mike Harrison

The primary coordinator and OFSTED re-inspection
Phil Gadsby and Mike Harrison

Coordinating the curriculum in the smaller primary school
Charles Easton, Jane Golightly and Mel Oyston, edited by Mick Waters

Coordinating the curriculum in the smaller primary school

Charles Easton
Jane Golightly
Mel Oyston
edited by Mick Waters

FALMER PRESS
Taylor & Francis Group

UK	Falmer Press, 11 New Fetter Lane, London, EC4P 4EE
USA	Falmer Press, Taylor & Francis Inc., 325 Chestnut Street, 8th Floor, Philadelphia, PA 19106

First published in 1999

A catalogue record for this book is available from the British Library

ISBN 0 7507 0700 3 paper

Library of Congress Cataloging-in-Publication Data are available on request

Jacket design by Carla Turchini

Typeset in 10/14pt Melior
Printed in Great Britain by
TJ International Ltd, Padstow, Cornwall

Contents

Part one
What are the managerial roles in the small school?

Part two
Staff expertise and development

Part three
Policy and planning

Part four
Monitoring the curriculum

Part five
Resources

Series editor's preface

This book has been prepared for primary teachers and headteachers in smaller primary schools and reflects the particular challenges of curriculum management and subject leadership within them. The authors define small schools not only in terms of numbers of pupils but also in their context including the size of neighbouring schools. However, by using case-study material from schools of 40 to 90 children where teachers have multi-subject multi-function roles many readers will be able to identify with the issues involved. The book forms part of a series of new publications that set out to advise teachers on the complex issues of improving teaching and learning through managing elements and aspects of the primary school curriculum.

Why is there a need for such a series? Most authorities recognise that the quality of primary children's work and learning depends upon the skills of their class teacher, not in the structure of management systems, policy documents or the titles and job descriptions of staff. Many today recognise that school improvement equates directly to the improvement of teaching so surely all tasks, other than imparting subject knowledge, are merely a distraction for the committed primary teacher.

Nothing should take teachers away from their most important role, that is, serving the best interests of the class of children in their care and this book, and the others in the series, does not wish to diminish that mission. However, the increasing complexity of the primary curriculum and society's expanding expectations, makes it very difficult for individual class teachers to keep up to date with every development. Within traditional subject areas there has been an explosion of knowledge and new fields introduced such as science, technology, design, problem solving and health education, not to mention the uses of computers. These are now considered entitlements for all primary children. Furthermore, we now expect all children to succeed at these studies, not just the fortunate few. All this has overwhelmed a class teacher system largely unchanged since the inception of primary schools.

Primary class teachers cannot therefore possibly be an expert in every aspect of the curriculum they are required to teach nor without help to provide for all their pupils. To whom can they turn for help? It is unrealistic to assume that such support will be available just from the headteacher whose responsibilities have grown ever wider since the 1988 Educational Reform Act. Constraints, including additional staff costs, and the loss of benefits from the strength and security of the class teacher system, militate against wholesale adoption of specialist or semi-specialist teaching. This is even less likely in small schools whose options in this regard are very limited. Help therefore has to come from exploiting the talents of teachers themselves, in a process of mutual support. Hence primary schools have chosen many and varied systems of consultancy or subject coordination which best suit the needs of their children and the current expertise of the staff. This book addresses the particular issues arising from this approach when schools have only a very small number of teachers.

Charles Easton, Jane Golightly, Mel Oyston and Mick Waters, emphasise the significance of management and coordination skills in the small school situation. The book has been written just after the standards for subject leadership have been published by the TTA and will be a useful complement to those considering their roles in improving curriculum provision. It offers practical guidance and insights for anyone in a small school who has a responsibility for ensuring that all pupils have access to the full curriculum, including teachers with an overall role in coordinating the whole or key stage curriculum and the deputy head and headteacher.

Leadership functions in primary schools have increasingly been shared with class teachers through the policy of coordination for the past twenty years, especially to improve the consistency of work in language and mathematics. Since then each school has developed their own system and the series recognises that each school will have a compromise between the ideal and the possible. Campbell and Neill (1994) show that by 1991 nearly nine out of every ten primary class teachers had such responsibility and the average number of subjects each was between 1.5 and 2.2 (depending on the size of school).

Each book in this series deals with specific issues whilst at the same time providing an overview of general themes in the management of the subject curriculum. The purpose of the series is to give practical guidance and support to teachers in particular what to do and how to do it. They each offer help on the production, development and review of policies and schemes of work; the organisation of resources; and developing strategies for improving the management of the curriculum and its implementation.

Mike Harrison, Series Editor
February 1999

Introduction

This book has been written essentially for the headteacher. However, other staff members may wish to dip into it from time to time.

Managing the whole school curriculum is the theme of this book, although the links with the totality of management will be evident. It is aimed at staff who have a multi-management role, usually including a range of subjects and duties, as Mel indicates:

> Being head of a very small school is a fascinating and rewarding experience. You have to be a jack of all trades: a master of the computer, a financial wizard, the ultimate classroom teacher etc. etc. who is prepared for any eventuality. At times you begin to wonder if having a qualification in plumbing or woodwork might be more useful than any teaching qualification. However, you have the distinct advantage among headteachers of being able to know your school, its pupils, staff and resources inside out. Your knowledge of every area of the curriculum will be confirmed as you will have direct involvement in the formation and delivery of every curriculum policy. As an almost full-time class teacher you are directly involved with putting theory into practice, you are a consumer of your own bright management ideas and therefore a quality control critic — if the reading record sheet you so lovingly designed takes hours to fill in and makes no sense when it is completed, you will be the first to know about it! You will be able to initiate change within your own school quickly and effectively and respond to changes in national policy rapidly. Small schools are fast on their feet and can be at the cutting edge of educational development.

Defining what is meant by being a small school is more complicated than it may at first appear, depending on the school context, such as the size of nearby schools. Small schools are often thought of as being rural but there are also many smaller urban schools. Any school, however, which describes itself as such may feel it requires curriculum management information which is more appropriate to its particular circumstances. This is the aim of this book, which uses two school case studies to illustrate the information. One is a two teacher school of 40 children where Mel is the headteacher, whilst the other is a four class school of 90 children where Jane is the headteacher. You may find the case study schools useful for reflecting on your own circumstances, and reinforcing your views and ideas.

Supporters of small schools often claim they have built-in advantages and disadvantages when developing the curriculum, many of which we have highlighted in the case studies in this book. The advantages of small schools have been reported from research, including OFSTED. These often include a strong family ethos and good relationships within the school and the wider community. They also have certain curriculum advantages such as their innovative, whole school approaches to the National Curriculum, experience of flexible teaching groups and use of a range of teaching strategies. Small schools will be in a strong position to use these skills within the Literacy Hour and Numeracy Strategy. However, there are also some specific challenges to those leading and working within the small school context. The provision of a broad and balanced curriculum, and the issue of subject leadership with a larger number of subjects and range of responsibilities and the challenge of teaching mixed age groups, for example, can seem daunting. However, with reflective management and a creative and determined approach these challenges can be turned into positives. This sometimes becomes clear when headteachers of small and large schools discuss issues and find they can have similar restrictions and encouragements.

Jane introduces the school where she is the headteacher:

The school is a rural primary school with 90 pupils. The main building is 150 years old, full of character and, although small, is a very attractive and much admired listed building. During the last eight years we have grown significantly in numbers and three outside classrooms provide accommodation for the pupils. The school currently has, including the headteacher, a 4.4 teaching staff with the head teacher teaching 0.6 each week.

Throughout this book, examples of formats and other materials from the case study schools and others are used. They were devised from the process or outcome of managing the curriculum in a small school. These materials are meant to be illustrative, rather than claim to be definitive works, as they have been designed to meet the particular need of one school. They could, however, form the starting points of your own designs, or complement the materials you already use. You may also wish to use this book alongside the more subject-specific handbooks in this series.

Part one

What are the managerial roles in the small school?

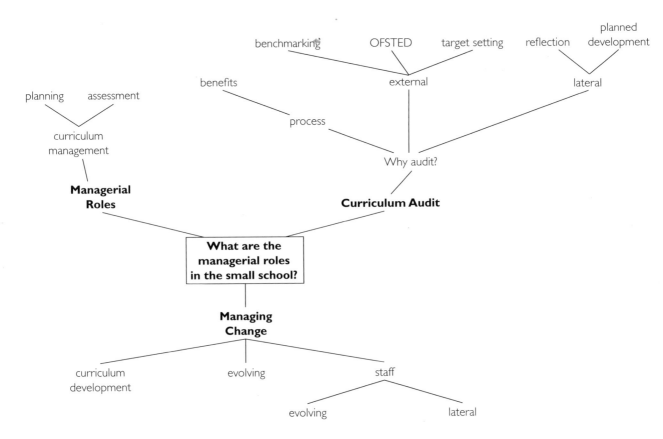

benchmarking   OFSTED   target setting   reflection   planned development

benefits   external   lateral

planning   assessment   process

curriculum management   Why audit?

Managerial Roles   **Curriculum Audit**

What are the managerial roles in the small school?

Managing Change

curriculum development   evolving   staff

evolving   lateral

| Chapter 1 | What are the managerial roles in the small school? |

In small schools most staff will have key curriculum managerial roles, and some individuals will have a whole range of them. This may be, for example, where a staff consists of a headteacher, perhaps a deputy headteacher, a special needs coordinator and a staff development officer. When allocating specific subject leader roles in such a situation you should first allocate the four core subjects, followed by linked foundation subjects. In this way the key subjects are given the status they require while the other subjects still have an advocate for them amongst the staff. Allocation of subject leader roles is discussed in more detail in Chapter 5.

In the small school situation, therefore, the staff may have subject leader responsibility for up to four or more subjects, depending on the number of staff. As it is not possible for a primary school teacher to have subject knowledge expertise in so many subjects, a subject leader could concentrate on providing:

- a strategic direction for the subject within the school, through providing inspiration, motivation and purpose;
- the monitoring and evaluation of the teaching and learning of the subject, including the use of targets and benchmarking;
- the management and leading of staff by providing support with planning, subject knowledge, assessment, recording systems and continuing professional development;

- monitoring of the effectiveness of the use of resources for the subject to meet the objectives and aims of the school and
- contributing to informing a range of audiences as to the standards of the subject and the targets for development.

Curriculum management

Having a clear understanding of the curriculum management role in a small school aids the delegation of tasks and provides a linked format to contribute to the many roles each individual may undertake. In this way, a range of tasks could be performed consecutively — such as the monitoring of literacy combined with the contributions to literacy made by the success of the code of practice for special educational needs. This is a key issue for a small school, allowing time to be used effectively, with duties reflecting the smaller numbers of individual teachers and children.

It is also useful to refer to the *Guidance on the Inspection of Nursery and Primary Schools* (HMSO, 1995) which provides a guide to the management of the curriculum. This is the criteria on which a school will be judged by OFSTED, and can be used to develop the role of everyone involved in curriculum management. The criteria within the guidance (pp. 76–9) are:

❜ *Is the curriculum balanced and broadly based? Does it promote pupils' intellectual, physical and personal development and prepare them for the next stage of education?*

Small schools have been shown to be able to meet these criteria because more emphasis can be given to each individual child. Even when the core subjects are given a greater emphasis, it should be possible to devise a subject structure which more suitably reflects the small school. In history, for example, the structure of concepts and skills could replace a content framework, thus overcoming the problem of split age ranges, mixed-age classes and annual class restructuring. It is also becoming increasingly accepted that some areas may demand a 'lighter touch' than others, so that the strengths of the teaching staff can be used effectively, while still providing a broad curriculum. The definition of a 'balanced' curriculum, however, is likely to continue to be affected by the pendulum effect of educational policy and schools will have to continually assess their current standing against the present requirements.

As the requirements of the National Curriculum change, the small school should be able to respond quickly due to the fewer individual staff involved. Try to be pro-active and think ahead where possible, so that developments and their required adjustments are made simultaneously, causing the least disruption. Many schools, for example, allocated time for Literacy and Numeracy Hours at the same time to prevent a second timetable review. Having a multiple managerial role should be used to its advantage, as there is less likelihood for disagreement over the time allocations for subjects and their position in the overall vision of the school.

Equality of access should rarely be an issue for a small school with its greater proportion of resources per pupil and the greater opportunities for children to mix and work with a range of children both in age and sex. This is a direct effect of the smaller numbers within each child's own age band. A school should, however, not be complacent over this issue.

In many small schools children will stay with a class teacher for more than one year. This allows the teachers to assess progress over one or more years, which can give a clearer picture of progress. The challenge is the range of development required in classes with more than one age group. This further emphasises the need for the curriculum in the small school to focus on developing concepts, skills and attitudes, which can be used to differentiate the content, especially when whole class teaching is used.

Planning

The greatest challenge for the small school is to ensure that the curriculum builds systematically on existing knowledge, understanding and skills. This is particularly important where classes contain more than one age group: thus providing continuity and progression of learning.

It is also a challenge for the producers of schemes of work and curriculum advisers to support the small school to devise systems in line with the support given to schools with single age group classes. Equal access for pupils should also be an issue for them, and every Local Education Authority with small schools should be able to advise on how new schemes of work will impact on the curriculum management of these schools.

See Chapters 7 and 9 for more information on planning the curriculum.

Assessment

Maintaining accurate assessment can be monitored through joint assessment meetings such as when reviewing the school's portfolio of assessed work. As there is less opportunity to work with staff teaching the same age range, it is a very suitable joint school activity, perhaps organised by the receiving secondary school.

Ensure that samples of work kept for individual children to exemplify attainment is stored in a manageable format, and preferably one which serves a multitude of uses — from reporting to parents to recording evidence of progress for the code of practice for special needs. It should reflect current progress, so the collection will involve removing and replacing work samples.

Future planning of the continuous programmes of study must be informed by assessment. In this way the differentiation required for each age band or achievement group within a class is carefully planned. This ensures that children make progress by building on previous learning, even when they share the same framework structure as children of different age groups and ability levels. Assessment of blocked work will be more summative, but an evaluation of the work will inform the planning the next time the subject features in the scheme of work.

See Chapter 8 for more on assessment.

Conclusion

The issues briefly raised in this chapter are discussed in the remainder of this book. It is a reflection of the nature of small schools that we have approached this in a practical format, such as by the use of the case study schools and the inclusion of exemplar materials. More specific subject issues are supported by other books within this series which, although not written specifically for small schools, will still be useful for teachers who work in them.

| Chapter 2 | The curriculum audit |

Why carry out a curriculum audit?

A curriculum audit may be inspired by internal reasons totally in the hands of the school. An example is on the appointment of a new headteacher when an audit is possibly the first major curriculum action — following the departure of the hired rubbish skip! An audit is a tool used to aid assimilation but can also help to develop relationships and support a working relationship among the staff. It is also a requirement of the Literacy and Numeracy Strategies.

At all times, however, it may be used as the means for encouraging an open management style allowing all staff to make contributions to the three year development plan. It can be the starting point of a shared vision for all connected with the management, including governors. In larger schools, where the role of the subject leader is an established feature, an annual audit by the subject leader is aimed at providing information on the achievement of targets as well as making future developments more manageable.

External pressures to carry out an audit often coincide with internal reasons. Clearly the demands of an inspection or target setting do create a climate in which everyone is focused on how well things are going. Providing policy documents and schemes of work for the school in preparation for and following an inspection is just one occasion when all the staff will regard an audit as necessary. Even streamlining the curriculum, especially the foundation subjects, will require an audit to ensure continuity and progression.

Jane explains the reasons for the audit process being used in her school:

Four years ago when I took up my post as head teacher, one of the first tasks we agreed to do was to examine the quality of the curriculum and to aim for familiarity with the Programmes of Study. We discovered that even in a school of three classes, which was the organisation of that time, there were uncertainties about the curriculum of different year groups.

As we each carry responsibility for more than one subject area, and to ensure that the targets of subjects for development was agreed overall, we began by taking an audit of the curriculum. This had the added bonus of addressing the curriculum aspect of the school development plan and, most importantly, all staff felt they had been involved in a priority area of school development.

It was decided to use staff development time for curriculum analysis and a timetable of meetings was drawn up to last over the first term. As a newly appointed head teacher who was taking responsibility for ensuring the delivery of the curriculum, I felt that the work was too important to be rushed and would also offer me valuable opportunities to learn about my new staff, how they worked together and the extent of curriculum expertise in the school.

No one was allowed to be a silent spectator. The outcome had to be a curriculum document that would work for our school and for each one of us in the classroom. All future meetings had agreed agenda items set at the end of meetings and, as curriculum leader, I circulated the minutes which became a useful starting point for the next meeting.

Initially, the task seemed quite overwhelming. How could five people ensure that all pupils cover all programmes of study at the appropriate level and that within this planned curriculum, differentiation and assessment were major features? After much discussion, which frequently went round in circles, we learned a valuable lesson. Start off in the area in which confidence and familiarity are greatest and progress from there. At the same time a decision was agreed to break down the work into manageable parts and set achievable targets e.g. listing the strengths and weaknesses in the delivery of information technology. Assessment and differentiation could wait until after we had dealt with the curriculum framework.

The staff were very honest when carrying out the audit. As the weeks progressed and we became involved in the exercise, issues began to emerge. For me, wearing both a curriculum and headteacher's hat, some of these were reassuring and some caused concern. For example, it emerged from the curriculum audit that due to accommodation problems we were having substantial difficulties in the delivery of the physical education curriculum. In order that the problems which arose did not overwhelm the staff and appear impossible, common sense acknowledged that many of the issues would take a considerable length of time to resolve, and outside factors beyond our control as curriculum leaders or as headteacher, would exert their influences.

The reasons for carrying out a curriculum audit is echoed by the experiences of Mel who explains his philosophy for carrying out an audit even in a very small school, where it might be assumed one was not required:

No matter how big or small a school or organisation is, the guiding principles for managing change and development, I believe, remain the same:
- decide **where** you are going;
- **when** you will get there;
- and **how** you are going to do it.

Before you can decide where you are going you must first look at where you are now. It is important to identify the positive aspects of your school, as well as areas ripe for development, as these will be the strengths on which progress will be built.

In order to move the school forward rapidly, an immediate audit was carried out which formed the starting points of the three year school development plan. Curriculum management is part of whole school development. The school development plan must include all aspects of its development not just the curriculum as all areas are interdependent on one another. For instance, it would be difficult to develop information technology through the purchase of new equipment if there was no money available to provide it because your budget was being taken up with repairs to the toilet block. The school must be seen as an entire organisation consisting of many interdependent parts.

The following are points to prepare before an audit exercise:
- establish whether the climate exists for an audit;
- decide who will be taking part;
- make sure everyone knows of new external developments;
- make relevant information available e.g. SATS results;
- use a system and format which are comfortable for all;
- involve all participants in recording;
- keep summarising and check understanding;
- give opportunities for all participants to speak and contribute and
- set time restrictions for the audit exercise.

Any audit will take time so it needs to be a worthwhile exercise. Some examples of the benefits for everyone were recorded by Jane:

The advantages of the audit far outweighed the disadvantages. Throughout the term and the process we began to work as a team and many benefits resulted. Some examples of these were:
- increased cooperation among staff;
- increased staff confidence;
- staff were involved in worthwhile and frank discussions about the curriculum;
- greater awareness of pressure between year groups and key stages;
- recognition of curriculum gaps;
- raised curriculum awareness;
- sharing expertise;
- increased curriculum familiarity;
- staff acknowledged curriculum strengths and weaknesses;
- issue of the quality, use and sharing of resources, was addressed and
- subject leaders gained greater awareness about the delivery of their subjects.

Perhaps, most importantly of all, was our agreement that the work on improving our understanding of the curriculum would influence our teaching and in turn improve the quality of standards we were striving to obtain.

However, at the same time as the curriculum strengths list was growing, the weaknesses list was also getting longer. One of the major issues in our school, as in many small schools, is the amount of subject responsibility which individual teachers carry. The audit sessions provided an ideal opportunity to review responsibilities and allow frank and open discussion. We all found these sessions so valuable that a decision was taken to ensure that each term we hold a review meeting to evaluate our work of that term. We still do this and it has been a most successful initiative.

Our areas of concern were not uncommon to both small and large schools. Alterations to the National Curriculum, the knowledge that OFSTED would be continually inspecting schools, and information from county training programmes had helped us recognise that classroom organisation, differentiation, policies, schemes of work, lack of subject expertise, provision for more and less able pupils; were all areas in which we wanted further professional development. Therefore, the curriculum audit helped us prioritise our in-school staff development programme, our participation in county courses and the advice we sought from the advisory service.

The process of a curriculum audit

There are established formats for carrying out an audit — such as the format contained in the literacy conference pack — which can be adapted to small school circumstances where a statistical analysis will be of less value. One method is for individuals to write down perceived strengths, short-term issues, and longer-term issues on colour-coded pieces of card. When the cards are gathered together, everyone looks for connections and sorts out different issues which should create a focused discussion in order to clear up any misunderstandings. The emerging themes should be recorded. This can then be used for a more thorough audit of the issues the staff would like to develop.

The tasks developed by SCAA now (QCA) in their booklet on planning the curriculum at Key Stages 1 and 2 offers a more formal audit, with an audit of time and other aspects of the curriculum. These include a decision on which programmes for each subject should be classed as blocked work and which is continuous work. Although not all programmes fit neatly into these categories they are a useful starting point for planning the long-term programme of work. Blocked work can be thought of as that which can be planned as a timed module of work, such as a content area in science. Continuous Programmes of Study can be thought of as the work which is drip fed to the children over their time in the school and is differentiated according to their present level of achievement.

If these tasks are used a very clear audit of the curriculum process will be achieved, even if the individual subjects will still require a more detailed audit. One management style would be to delegate the leading of the tasks to different staff members who would then each have a manageable amount of preparation.

A carefully prepared and uniform format for a subject audit would ensure that each area is looked at in the same way, so aspects cannot be overlooked, and staff become familiar with the process. This will help resolve issues of time spent on an audit and give confidence to everyone who leads a particular subject audit. The uniform format could include resources, subject knowledge and current practice among its items.

The format chosen should reflect the preferred system of working as Mel's and Jane's experiences illustrate:

Mel:

It was important that as many people contributed to the audit process as possible in order to get a balanced view of the school from a variety of standpoints and interests. Sheets of paper were pinned to a staff room wall each with a heading of an area for development:
- school document
- curriculum development
- administration
- home and school liaison and reporting
- resources — curriculum
- resources — other
- staff development
- governors
- marketing — school image and community links
- financial

Staff, parent helpers and governors added items to each list whenever an idea occurred to them and the lists soon became a bank of ideas about where the school was at that moment, along with suggestions for future development. Sometimes the things added to the lists were self-apparent, a gut reaction, sometimes issues were raised that have been a personal concern of people for some time but they had not had a forum to voice their ideas.

Observation of children as they performed tasks and interacted with each other was an immediate indicator of social and moral development as well as demonstrating attitudes to teaching and learning.

Resources were sorted and organised. Careful note was made on a resources list in the staff room of any obvious gaps in the provision of books or other equipment.

Each school carries its own tradition of acknowledged strengths, often musical, dramatic or sporting, and it was important to identify and maintain these areas. The most notable strength of our very small school was the way in which all children had access to the curriculum and all children had an opportunity to play a leading role. Every child takes a major role in dramatic productions, every child represents the school in a sports team etc. These opportunities enable children to achieve success beyond their expectations. Recognition of this approach was to form the corner-stone of our school ethos.

I felt it was important to involve children in the audit. Their views and opinions provided an important insight into how they saw the school functioning, what they valued about the school, what they expected from the school and what they regarded as areas of potential change.

Other obvious strengths included strong community support, close contact with parents, good staff communication and the ability to react swiftly.

All these points were recorded on the appropriate list as a picture of the school emerged.

This was a very tentative approach to a whole school audit made by a newly appointed head teacher in a new school in an environment very different to anything I had experienced before. Since then I have employed a variety of different alternatives to discover where the school is at in terms of achievement and standing in the community. A combination of these could be used to carry out an initial audit of the strengths and weaknesses of a school.

Standardised testing, including SATS, over a period of time has revealed areas of success or concern. The outcome of an inspection provides its own agenda of strengths and weaknesses. Teacher appraisal and classroom observation, although not approaches often used during the initial stages of a headship appointment, are useful tools in understanding how the delivery of the curriculum matches the intended aims and ethos of the school. You can make use of your local education services by inviting a curriculum advisory teacher to investigate a specific subject area, looking at policy resources or delivery. Carrying out a survey of parental opinion can be a very revealing exercise and one we have used regularly to monitor and evaluate our progress. Employing the assistance of a visiting experienced professional to act as a neutral observer can provide an objective opinion of a school's standing.

Several weeks and many additions later, the lists were taken from the walls and assessed.

Jane:

At the first meeting we agreed on a format for the process. Previous experience of the management of meetings had taught me that it is very easy for staff to deviate from the point so we agreed that a strengths and weaknesses format would ensure we remembered the focus and be an easier method of recording the discussion. Perhaps one of my major advantages, and one that is easy to forget, was that the staff wanted to participate in this exercise. They could see the long-term benefits and felt it would develop our school. There was no necessity on my part to cajole or persuade reluctant teachers to take part. Therefore from the first meeting we were able to begin constructive work.

A large pot of tea, plenty of biscuits and many sheets of paper became the required resources for staff development sessions that first autumn term. In order to ensure that everyone participated, each staff member took responsibility for recording some of the discussion and reminding us of the main points at the next meeting.

Planned development

As in many schools, the results of the audit in Mel's school formed the major element of the three year development plan. This allowed Mel to prioritise developments, cost them, and

School development plan for autumn half term

School documentation		
Curriculum development (whole school policies)		
Administration		
Home/school liaison and reporting		
Assessment		
Recording and record keeping		
Private sector liaison		
Resources curriculum		
Resources other		
Staff development		
Governors		
Marketing/school image		
Financial		

link them to other school developments. It has the added advantages of encouraging the support of outside agencies including LEA officers, and can form the basis of bids for building development initiatives or extra resources funding. Everyone involved should be more willing to invest time and energy into achieving the targets of the development plan because they were instrumental in drawing them up. Any work delegated will be understood by those carrying out the task because they would have been party to the decision. Targets and the development plan should carry a high status amongst all who were participants in the audit process.

The format used in Mel's school is included to show how the audit developed into the school's development plan.

There were many strengths recognised on which to build and many areas of need identified. These needs were prioritised and formed the basis of a three year development plan. This development plan was to drive the re-shaping of the school — it had to be ambitious and demanding and yet be realistic. The initial three year plan was set out on grid sheets using the same heads as the audit list:

There was a sheet for each term (see example above) onto which expected outcomes were written, for example: behaviour policy completed, new carpet purchased, SATS carried out etc. Time slots were indicated on a plan as end dates by which time the items should be completed. It was important to include all school and staff commitments on a plan.

The value of a plan is to make the whole process of school development manageable and to provide a clear demonstration of where you are now, what you intend to do and when it will be done. The plan has enabled us to:

- set a sensible diary to develop the school's documents and policy statements;
- manage the school's budget efficiently by targeting areas of spending;
- plan a coherent system of staff training and
- communicate the school's developments and aspirations to parents.

A development plan should be a working document which not only tells you what you should be doing now but also justifies why you are not doing certain things at the moment either.

Once a plan was published and put into action, the headings from the grid plan (see outline above) were used as side headings for the headteacher's report to governors. We all knew where we were going, what we needed to achieve it and when. The headteacher's

School development plan Autumn half term 1995		
School documentation	Review severe weather policy Prepare whole year planning diary for staff room	Fire drill carried out and recorded (children reminded of procedure) DP to office Collective worship policy prepared OFSTED documentation prepared
Curriculum development (whole school policies)	*Hand for Spelling* introduced Possible content of maths policy discussed SEN support trialled STEPS maths materials introduced Teaching and Learning — policy written	Rugby coaching sessions with development officer Joint curr. planning for next term — carried out Work on drafting Eng Writing Policy begins Quality and Expectations — policy written
Administration	Admin policy file created Health and Safety policy completed Pre OFSTED inspection by advisory team	Office layout reviewed
Home/school liaison and reporting	Behaviour policy shared with parents Parent/teacher interviews (afternoon/eve.) Daily school/home communication reviewed (home book etc.)	School's Framework for the management of the curr. shared with parents Seek preferences from parents concerning focus of curr. evening in Spring term
Assessment	Baseline assessment carried out	Assessment policy reviewed in the light of INSET course
Recording and record keeping		Record keeping reviewed in the light of INSET course
Pri/Sec Liaison		Y6 parents invited to secondary school
Resources curriculum	Review DT resources in the light of advisory teacher's visit	
Resources other	Purchase of outdoor adventure equipment TV/video purchased for KS1 room Refurbishment of staff room completed (chairs and curtains)	Visit of 'The Apprentice Sorcerer' play — joint venture with N School
Staff development Governors	Headteacher appraisal begins INSET — Classroom Management	INSET — Action Planning Post OFSTED INSET — Visually Impaired Children INSET — Assessment and Recording INSET — Textiles INSET — Counselling Skills AGM + SEN Gov training
Marketing/school image	School photographer Autumn Event Harvest Festival Parents of prospective pupils contacted Series of inter school sports events organised Regular display of work set up in village hall	Charity supported — 3rd World Disco Carol service whole school Y1/2 production
Financial	Money div. between depts. in budget review & update	Budget situation reviewed

report became a progress report on the shared goals we had set for the school.

In the busy life in an ever changing world of education we often forget to stop and consider our achievements. It is important to value your successes. Set up a sort of public mile stone chart on which achievements can be recorded, shared and celebrated.

After the initial three year development period the next step was to organise a cycle of monitoring and development which would ensure existing policies were discussed regularly, kept up to date and evaluated for success while allowing chosen themes to be focused on during a year.

Summary

- Audit for continuity and progression and managing change and development.
- Consider using established formats and delegate tasks.
- Be flexible in the use of formats and systems to reflect current school circumstances.
- Decide on the participants and their level of involvement.
- Plan a cycle of curriculum review which complements the process of creating the school's development plan.
- Celebrate achievements.

Chapter 3

Managing change

Just when everything seems to be planned and in place — a sensible time scale for school development is in operation and things are running smoothly — something happens to rock the boat. It could be a staff change or illness, a change of National Curriculum policy or a proposed inspection, and it must be dealt with. Staff change may not come very often in a small school but when it does it tends to have major consequences — for some small schools, one member of staff leaving represents a 50 per cent staff turn over.

Change and development

In recent years schools have become expert at managing change; even being able to make the process of change itself a positive aspect. Most changes are more accurately described as 'developments' as they refine or extend aspects of school life that already exist. The Literacy Hour, for example, may require alterations to the timetable and class organisation, but uses skills and teaching styles that teachers are already familiar with. Managing this type of change often requires in-service for the staff, and the purchase of resources. A positive management style is needed to support teachers, especially if the process begins by reviewing what staff already are doing.

A development plan should be seen as the school's intentions for development but needs to be flexible enough to respond to new circumstances. This is why a three year plan is put into action annually by a management plan which reviews what has and has not been achieved and what changes to the long-term aspects are therefore required. When beginning a new development plan try to gather as much information about external developments as possible, then link these with the school's own aspirations. An example is the preparation required for inspection and the action plan which follows. A reflective approach to change can be seen in Jane's school:

Events which enforce change frequently lead to evaluation and reflection. This applies to the curriculum as in other areas. A major change in our school was the move from a three class school with a mixed Key Stage 1 and 2 class to a four class school. This is an expensive change and the results in progress and achievement have to merit it, therefore the process is being carefully monitored by staff and governors. It required an audit of curriculum delivery throughout the whole school.

The work is on-going, involving restructuring the Programmes of Study. At the same review the curriculum for 4-year-old children was matched to the Desirable Learning Outcomes for this age group. This also required some financial support.

The process of any changes involves methodical and detailed planning and some issues may continue to be unresolved for a significant period. It is important to be realistic and accept that a longer time scale and financial support will resolve it.

Opportunity to reflect on the successes of managing change is most important and as review meetings are part of our staff development time we are now better at expressing opinions and arriving at solutions which resolve difficulties. At the end of the first term of the change to the class structure, a meeting was held to discuss the influence of the re-organisation on curriculum delivery. Within Key Stage 1 there are two very small classes and the progress of pupils is being carefully monitored. The main benefits to curriculum are the additional time to extend learning for all abilities and the effects on planning. At the same time as recognising advantages we attempt to take an overall view and discuss areas which as individually or collectively we have concerns about. Following discussion it is agreed that work has to continue to be developed, targets will be set e.g. to increase opportunities for subject leaders to spend time in other classes sharing expertise.

Changes in staffing

Managing a change in staffing often starts with thinking about the appointment. This is when a decision about the job specification needs to be made. Should a post be advertised asking for: a particular subject specialist? a teacher who favours a particular teaching style? or a specific personality such as a completer of work to complement a staff who are expert at beginning initiatives? Most small schools will advertise for a teacher who is able to show general expertise across the subject range, with perhaps a desirable additional specific expertise. This could be an expertise chosen by the school either as a single subject such as information technology; or a group of subjects such as creative arts; or left to the candidates to identify. Deciding on the specification will depend on the staff remaining in the school and the potential quality of the candidates. You might choose to employ a sound general teacher who can contribute to the style and ethos of the school rather than a teacher chosen on single subject specialism alone — the significance of being able to play a piano should not be more important than the judgment of the candidate's ability as a class teacher!

Perhaps the biggest change of all is when a new headteacher is appointed. In both our case study schools there has been much emphasis on curriculum development since the heads were appointed. The balance is to:

■ decide what needs immediate attention, for example, health and safety and the attitude to teaching and learning;
■ decide which strengths to build on, ensuring that others are not lost;
■ decide what developments can be longer-term issues.

The vehicle for this is the curriculum and school audit which provides the structures required for development planning. A three year development plan allows the newly appointed headteacher to feel he or she can pace the school development, while retaining the school's strengths.

Any new appointment should bring with it an induction programme. Using a mentor can be beneficial, especially if the appointed person is a newly qualified teacher, together with a monitor who is likely to be a governor. The aim of an induction programme is to allow a teacher to have a gradual introduction to the school so that he or she is not overwhelmed with the mass of information. They should also structure the involvement in management so that everyone realises the aim of the first weeks is to become aware of the curriculum, organisation and children of the class they are teaching. Eventually the programme may lead to becoming a subject leader or holder of another post of responsibility. The advantage of distributing the programme amongst staff and governors is that expectations will be known and everyone feels empowered by contributing to the induction. Even a new headteacher would benefit from such a programme — although the space for a gradual introduction to responsibilities will be difficult to achieve!

An induction programme for a newly appointed deputy head teacher of a small school of 140 children is included as an example below.

Induction Programme
Deputy Headteacher

Appointed: 15/10/98   In post: 1/1/99

Aims:
1   To aid the transition from the present post to the new
2   To allow the teaching role to take precedence during the initial period
3   To plan for an incremental development of managerial experience and responsibility

Relevant information:
1   Information generated for the appointment
2   Policy documentation
3   'Inherited' planning systems and resources
4   Generic Job Description for class teachers and deputy headteachers
5   School development and management plans

Relevant background:
Experience as a class teacher and subject manager, as well as managerial INSET.

The programme

Pre-post
1   Time spent in school during the interview
2   One and a half days in school following the appointment
3   Liaison with AP to plan the work in the cooperative teaching situation

---

4 Liaison with HT to initiate the aims and content of this programme
5 Work on mid-term plans within the school's long-term framework to be produced with communication by post
6 Agreement on music and mathematics for subject management

Term 1

Focus for first half term: Class teacher
1 The main aim is to relate to the children of the class and school, and to use this as a means of establishing effective relationships with the staff
2 To continue with the established work pattern
3 Review the class arrangements by half-term and liaise with AP for any developments

NB To also make an immediate impact on the school and to establish credentials among parents, will be the use of musical expertise in extra-curricular activities.

Focus for half term: Class teacher and subject management
1 Establishment of agreed developments within the class through liaison with A
2 Subject review conducted by HT with staff liaison through staff meetings
3 Organising subject manager files

Term 2

Focus: Preparation for extending managerial responsibilities.
1 Attending Curriculum and Building/Health and Safety Governor committees prior to being fully co-opted onto these committees
2 Working with present post-holder prior to assuming responsibility for school-wide management post by negotiation (e.g. SENCO, SDO)
3 Day visit arranged to the Secondary School to develop role of KS2/3 liaison teacher

Term 3

1 Writing of the job specification
2 Contributing to the development of a new three year development plan, especially in the areas of the curriculum and building
3 Open invitation to join the staffing/finance committee
4 HT to work with DH on budgetary issues
5 HT to produce a version of the budget for the following year for comparison etc.

Evaluation

1 Production of relevant job specification
2 DH to report on the programme to the governing body

Development

Appraisal in Term 4

Budget

1 2 days' supply available in the first term (school budget)
2 Use of GEST budget: Minimum 3 days' supply allocated from 98/99 budget
3 Seek to establish some element of non-contact through the school budget either by part-time teacher support or a fixed amount of supply allocation, in the 98/99 school budget.

Another tool which could be used alongside the induction programme is a staff handbook which contains simple practical information such as:

■ a list of personnel, including governors;
■ the times of the school day and a timetable;
■ a list of central resources and how they are used;
■ guidance on which policies should be read immediately, e.g. health and safety, special needs etc.;
■ a general offer of support and help;
■ information about what to do in the event of being unable to attend school; and
■ a school plan.

Even in a small school there is so much information to accommodate that a staff handbook can be the starting point for the newly appointed member of staff to raise questions. If received when the job is offered, newly appointed staff can arrive even on the first visit with questions and a possible observation schedule, and begin to feel part of the school immediately. A staff handbook can also be used for new supply teachers who could refer to them so they feel confident and are able to teach without being worried they are missing important features of the day.

In Jane's school the newly appointed teacher would be guided into post:

Changes of teaching personnel bring with them the issue of ensuring coverage is not detrimentally affected. New staff, supply teachers, students and newly qualified teachers are offered a mentoring process which allows them time to gain familiarity with the school's approach to curriculum delivery.

I have found that it is extremely difficult to spend specific time in another teacher's classroom and equally difficult for the new member of staff to become familiar with everything which is part of school policy. Therefore I developed a mentoring procedure which can be adapted to meet individual requirements, e.g. a new teacher with experience will require a different programme to a newly qualified teacher. Through a series of planned and timed meetings over a period of time I encouraged new staff to become familiar with the following documents:

- school development plan
- planning documents
- procedures for staff development
- policy statements
- schemes of work
- behaviour and discipline policy
- school aims and objectives
- resources and their purchase
- health and safety
- educational visits
- parents in school
- special educational needs

The above is not exhaustive but by being specific about the agenda for each meeting and keeping to the date and time, new staff quickly become familiar with school procedures and most importantly have the total attention of the headteacher allowing them to discuss issues and any concerns.

Summary

- Change is best managed as a development from existing practice.
- Development planning should be able to adapt to changes.
- Newly appointed staff require an induction programme.

Part two | Staff expertise and development

Chapter 4
Staff expertise and
staff development

Chapter 5
The role of the subject leader

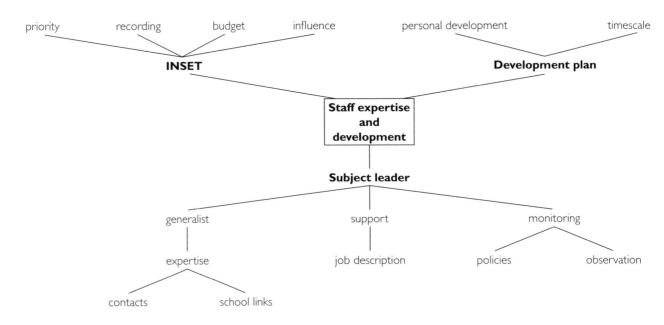

priority   recording   budget   influence   personal development   timescale

INSET   **Development plan**

Staff expertise and development

Subject leader

generalist   support   monitoring

expertise   job description   policies   observation

contacts   school links

Chapter 4

Staff expertise and development

Staff expertise

The level of subject expertise is often thought to be a problem in smaller primary schools, where staff may have to be 'experts' in many subject areas. However, recent OFSTED inspection evidence has shown that subject expertise in small primary schools compares favourably with that in larger schools. There are particular subjects which schools have traditionally thought to be more specialised, such as music. These specialisms, however, seem to be being successfully provided by looking beyond the school. Teachers can, for example, be encouraged to use the Internet to find information from the 'Virtual Teacher Centres' or by use of e-mail to link with other schools and teachers to share expertise and information. Some schools have even begun to experiment with video conferencing to provide modern foreign language lessons to children in small schools who would not otherwise receive them.

The focus on literacy, numeracy, science and information communication technology as the core subjects, may benefit smaller schools in the development of subject expertise, which should be able to concentrate on improving teaching and learning in these areas.

The perceived challenges of small schools with regard to staff expertise are:

- each teacher has to lead more subjects;
- some subjects may have no natural subject leader on the staff; and
- there are fewer staff to share ideas, experiences and support.

In order to manage these, every school will need to develop creative solutions, such as seeking voluntary help, perhaps from a parent, or by employing more part-time teachers to the same equivalent time, each of whom may offer different expertise. If a particular subject leader requires more support, this can be obtained from the subject-specific handbooks, which form part of this series.

In attempting to manage every subject the school should begin by asking what they can already do well. This then forms the starting point for development, building on existing strengths and knowledge. Areas where more problems are perceived can then be sectioned into small steps of development, making in-service and advice more focused and effective.

In all subjects the notion of subject expertise should be discussed and defined with the staff, as the lack of some subject knowledge may not be recognised. This needs to be managed in a structured way, however, so as not to create a crisis in confidence and overwhelm staff with too many in-service requirements. The most appropriate times are during the review of subject policy and schemes of work as part of the planned cycle of review of the curriculum; following an audit of a specific subject, or in the wake of an inspection which might have highlighted a lack of subject knowledge for specific subjects. Equally, check that staff are not over-estimating the level of subject knowlege required, causing a lack of confidence.

In all discussions of subject expertise it needs to be emphasised continually that there are two basic expert requirements for successful teaching: subject knowledge *and* professional teaching skills. The latter are the abilities necessary for teaching all subjects, developed through initial training, in-service training and experience. There should be a realistic approach to develop subject knowledge which, for future generations of teachers, may be less of an issue if the requirements for qualifying as a teacher under the Teacher Training Agency arrangements are successful.

Just as there are perceived disadvantages in small schools, however, there are advantages. For example:

- the expertise of one member of staff may cover the whole of a key stage or perhaps one-quarter of the whole staff;
- staff exchange between classrooms can be managed fairly easily, as any expertise offered will not keep a teacher from their own class for many periods;
- a large proportion of any in-service will be first hand, so a course for subject knowledge involving one teacher could cover the whole of a key stage.

Mel's descriptions continue the theme of managing both potential difficulties and advantages:

It is a particular challenge within a small school to ensure the continued and effective professional development of staff. The children may be with a teacher for the whole of a key stage. The teacher needs to understand the particular needs of each age group and ability level within that key stage as well as acquiring a sound knowledge of the curriculum areas.

In our particular LEA each school can buy into an annual service level agreement which offers a sliding scale of course attendance days and access to advisory staff. This represents good value for the small school as even at the cheapest basic entry level at least eight course days are available for our two staff.

The notion that small schools cannot provide the necessary expertise to deliver the full range of the National Curriculum is largely misplaced. Small schools can and do cope with the demands of a broad curriculum. Staff training in small schools can be very direct and efficient as unlike larger schools they do not face the difficult challenge of ensuring the expertise of a teacher with a particular subject specialism influences the delivery of this curriculum area in every class. There exists in a small school the opportunity to attend in-service training courses across the whole curriculum rather than rely on the second hand experience of listening to the post-course report of a subject leader during a staff meeting.

The teacher in a very small school has to be master of a wide range of talents, not only may you have to take the football team but also you have to provide the accompaniment for singing in assembly. We are fortunate in our school that the experience and expertise of our two staff complement each other and between us we can cover all the curriculum areas and advise each other on the finer points of subject detail. A shared enthusiasm for music was a tremendous plus. However, it was important not to become complacent. An effective staff development plan had to be introduced to ensure we kept up to date on curriculum and management issues.

As we all have to teach every National Curriculum subject, it is argued that we all require training in all areas of the curriculum. Having a coherent system of staff training was vital in order to enable the effective delivery of the curriculum within our school. Both teachers had to extend their expertise in each curriculum area. This sounds a daunting and formidable task but in a two-teacher school there is far more opportunity to allow teachers to attend courses to develop their professional skills. For the cost of one day's supply cover and annual subscription to the LEA service level agreement half the staff could go on a geography course, for example, and a whole key stage has been updated!

In larger schools there is a broader base from which to draw examples of good practice. It was necessary for us to organise visits to other schools to allow staff the opportunity to sample the approaches to teaching and classroom management employed by other professionals.

The selection of in-service courses takes place at the end of the financial year. The subject matter of the course chosen is largely dictated by priorities identified in the school development plan. For instance, in a year in which physical education as been designated a development area, courses on games, gymnastics, swimming and dance may be selected for attendance. The atmosphere of cooperation and support that can exist in a very small school generates regular discussion and reflection on issues of teaching and learning. Staff appraisal of both the headteacher and teacher provides another basis of selecting appropriate in-service courses.

The greatest strength of any school is the quality of its teachers; this is even more relevant in a small school where a teacher is responsible for an entire key stage. Staff training is therefore a major investment and should be to the forefront of any school development planning and budget allocation.

Staff development

Mel has emphasised the importance of in-service training to develop the expertise and professional skills of teachers, and that this should be a structured programme linked to the development plan. This separate staff development plan, which is part of the development plan, allows for some element of individual development, as well as being consistent with the general development plan. Another approach is to devise subject development plans, which we consider in Chapter 5.

It may appear that teachers in small schools have to attend more in-service courses. While this might be the case, there are advantages that should be encouraged through successful management:

■ A larger proportion of the teacher's in-service training is first hand.
■ Any in-service undertaken will affect a larger proportion of children's learning.
■ The requirements of feedback for other teachers may be less.

Whatever its size, every school needs to manage the in-service training carefully to maximise its potential to have a direct effect on the quality of teaching and learning in the school. Effective planning ensures the best use is made of limited standards funding and the following qualities are a feature:

■ a managed programme which is consistent with the development plan;
■ opportunities are provided for personal professional development;
■ advice is actively sought; and
■ there is time to follow up in-service, perhaps by discussions with the whole staff.

Staff meetings are the most common type of follow up to in-service courses. While every school will aim to manage these meetings well, including starting and finishing them on time, in a small school meetings will be shorter due to the different logistics. Discussions will also be more intensive for each teacher. The programme of staff meetings should also include time for reflection and liaison so that short-term issues are addressed as well as those relating to long-term development.

Jane explains the process of devising a structure of staff development and discusses the issues of staff expertise in smaller schools:

Planning a staff development programme was part of the process of writing the school development plans and budget management. The starting point to develop an organised and beneficial programme was to audit current expertise. This scrutiny was taken in the form of strengths and weaknesses with everyone contributing freely about the areas in which they have confidence and those which need further advice and support. The staff, with the exception of the newly qualified member, has a broad experience and has been involved in the National Curriculum from its introduction. They are well established as a team and have confidence in seeking advice from each other.

In acknowledging that 5 teachers have to cover the development of the National Curriculum subjects and religious education, and other areas such as personal and social development, a principal objective from staff development is to maximise to its advantage the current expertise in school and to use standards funding to advance both personal and school growth. Following the audit there were clear indications of the areas which had to be addressed. These areas were then divided into two columns, individual and school, and each point was allocated to either one or the other. Following this they were ordered into priority and at the completion of this work a whole staff development structure had been agreed. This programme was the result of in-depth discussion spread over half a term.

From the programme, a plan of action was drawn up which was planned and costed within the school development plan and budget. A variety of sources would be used to provide training e.g. county courses, advisory service support and advice, national and county projects, local university courses, appraisal, visiting speakers and colleagues, in-school support and cooperative work. Initially, expectations of in-school work were too great and from experience the term's programme has been shortened allowing time for unexpected events or for planning on-going school occasions such as Harvest Festival, etc.

The planning of in-service development has become part of an integral term review. At these, staff reflect on the term and normal practice is to set targets for the following term. An example target could be to improve the use of the school library. The staff must agree targets, which have to be achievable and beneficial. These and the previous identified tasks ensure that the programme is continuing to be relevant to all staff. The summer term review has as its central focus the development programme for the coming year with the appointing of activities to specific terms and session leaders.

Throughout the academic year a cross-section of activities will be addressed and a detailed schedule of work is drawn up which will range from writing a curriculum policy to dissemination of in-service training. The headings shown below are used and the list of staff development is given to individual staff and displayed on the staff room notice board before the end of the previous term. Advantages of completing this work before the end of the term are that the staff has firm ideas about the areas they wish to cover and alterations to order of completion can take place. Secondly an agenda for training days can be set using those tasks which require maximum time and sustained concentration. Thirdly, planning in advance allows for visiting speakers, colleagues, support services etc. to be booked early. Informing staff in advance reinforces the message that in-school training is taken seriously.

Staff development programme		
Date	Area to be developed	Staff involved

The schedule above is dated in order of work and ticked off when completed. Tasks which were not completed are re-assigned to another term.

The provision for developing curriculum expertise is met through attendance at external courses. However, the limited standards funding has meant that when curriculum priorities are to be addressed the staff member who attends must be prepared to offer full feedback to the other staff. The decision about which courses to attend is related to the school development plan. The amount of courses we would like to attend is always greater than funding allows, therefore, the priority list and target setting of the term reviews become the decisive factors but the main aim is to provide a broad and balanced programme of support and development.

Records of individual attendance at in-service courses are retained in school. These have proved worthwhile when evaluating the staff development plan and at meetings between the staff and headteacher, when personal matters such as job applications and appraisal are discussed. The format is simple and takes seconds to complete. (See example below.)

Details of in-service training

Name
Place   Subjects   Date

We also have a form to complete following in-service, which acts as a memory aid when discussed by the individual with the head-teacher. The advantages of having this format are twofold: the teacher has an opportunity to reflect on the course and the most effective way of sharing information; and secondly it allows the headteacher to monitor and evaluate the success of in-service.

Staff development

Course attended:
Name:
Date:
Course leader:
Brief summary of content:

Personal evaluation of the course:

Targets: 1
             2
             3

The teacher keeps a copy of the completed form and a second is kept in the in-service training file. By ensuring that attended courses are followed up, value for money is obtained and results on teaching and learning can be monitored.

Summary

- Define which aspects of a subject may require development.
- Start from the sections of the programmes of study for a subject for which there is subject knowledge.
- Seek creative ways to cover subject knowledge.
- Structure in-service work to allow development consistent with the school development plan but which also allows individual professional development.
- When appointing new staff the knowledge gained may contribute to selecting personnel.

The role of the subject leader

Adapting to the role

The Teacher Training Agency supports the development of subject leaders, but the model best fits larger schools where an individual may have only one or two subjects to manage. Smaller schools therefore need to develop a system which can work for them.

The Teacher Training Agency has developed National Standards specifically for the subject leader (TTA, 1998) describing the 'core purpose' of the subject leader as:

❝ *To provide professional leadership and management of a subject to secure high quality teaching, effective use of resources and improved standards of learning and teaching for all pupils.*

Whilst this seems more relevant to teachers leading a single subject, the booklet then outlines the TTA's criteria for effective leadership and management. This list is reassuring for the teacher who leads a number of subjects, as it allows an interpretation that is more suitable for the smaller numbers of pupils and staff involved:

a. Pupils show sustained improvement in subject knowledge, understanding and skills, at a level appropriate to their age and level of development. They are well prepared for tests and maintain a purposeful attitude.

b. Teachers work together as a team, have high expectations and teach subjects effectively.
c. Parents are well informed.
d. Senior managers understand the needs of the subject to inform decision-making.
e. Other adults and external agencies are informed and make appropriate contributions.

A subject leader in the smaller school can use this list as a measure of their own effectiveness. The smaller numbers involved means that the list can be applied to individuals rather than cohorts, as every child will be known and probably taught by each subject leader. Any evaluation may identify areas for development, such as information for parents, which may be applicable to several subjects, so that subject and management tasks can be combined. Applying the list to a subject could be the start of a monitoring or liaison exercise.

The National Standards for Subject Leaders can be used to structure the role within a smaller school. Each subject area requires:
1. Professional, rather than subject, knowledge and understanding.
2. Leadership and management skills.

Professional knowledge and understanding common to all subjects includes, for example, the role of ICT within the subject; the requirements of the Code of Practice for Special Educational Needs; and how literacy and numeracy can be developed within many subjects. There is also the knowledge and understanding of the management within the school, such as how resources are allocated, and the role of the governors. In most smaller schools this knowledge should be more easily available to every staff member than in larger schools.

Management and leadership skills include:
- dealing sensitively with people;
- creating clear aims;
- thinking creatively and reflectively;
- making decisions;
- leading meetings.

When leading more than one subject, teachers will need to develop specific subject knowledge across a range of subjects. But this should be viewed as a long-term issue, requiring INSET and other support, as well as a clear analysis of the level of expertise required of subject knowledge. This is not to belittle the issue but to reinforce the position of the generic skills just described, which can be developed and then applied to all subjects as a central aspect of being a subject leader. Management training for everyone, such as the running of effective meetings, would be very efficient in the development of a school's curriculum.

In Mel's school, it was decided that the usual interpretation of the subject leader's role was not viable, as each of the two teachers would have so many subjects to lead, and instead chose to share tasks as they arose on the development plan. The small number of staff facilitates this:

> We have chosen not to have curriculum leaders. We all carry the shared responsibility of maintaining continuity and progression in all curriculum areas. During curriculum policy discussions the teacher who has the greatest subject knowledge in that particular area takes the lead. The ordering and management of resources is a joint responsibility. We wished to open up the curriculum; there seemed little point in dividing it up into two halves.
>
> In a two-teacher school the children will probably be with the same teacher for an entire key stage. Each teacher needs to be aware of the particular needs of each age group within that key stage in each area of that curriculum. Each teacher needs to develop an interest in every subject. In our very small school both teachers coordinate everything.

The advantage of developing the role of the subject leader in slightly larger schools or, if it is suitable, even very small schools is that there may be opportunities to delegate some responsibilities and to give staff experience which may contribute to their career opportunities, such as building up expertise and organising the in-service training for the school. In small schools, however, the role of the subject leader may need to be adaptable, and you may wish to develop a more flexible approach than the single subject leader found in large schools. Use opportunities to combine tasks for subjects, such as the planning formats, to support teachers who are leading more than one subject. Think about involving leaders with the following rather than just specific subject responsibilities:

■ leading tasks, which have been identified by the development plan;
■ grouping areas which cross subject boundaries;
■ sharing out subjects to be reviewed during the particular year; and
■ linking with other local schools to share joint subject leadership.

For example, when leading tasks identified by the development plan where the subject may be a central concern — if the school was developing information technology, for example — the subject leader could concentrate on developing a strategy for in-service training, including raising subject knowledge, whilst funding could be organised by the headteacher and governors. Crossing curriculum boundaries may involve one leader for special needs and assessment while another could be leading planning, continuity and progression. In this way a cooperative approach could be devised for each subject or development idea but with delegated roles and responsibilities for all.

Sharing out subjects for the year should result in an equal distribution of development work amongst the staff, but does not deal with the issue of subject knowledge. This is where a school needs to be clear on the level of expertise the role requires as well as being creative in seeking support or joining with other schools who are reviewing the same subject. Some schools are working together to produce policies and schemes of work which can then be adapted to the needs of each individual school. Joint in-service may be more readily supported by the local officers, or limited standards funding budgets joined to buy in trainers. Some schools have even confederated to provide joint teaching for areas such as investigative science or sports, although this is restricted by transport costs.

Whatever model you use for subject leadership, make sure that the system chosen is used while it is useful but is adapted when circumstances change. The reassurance is that inspection evidence has not highlighted small schools as being unable to deliver a broad and balanced curriculum meeting the requirements of the National Curriculum. In slightly larger schools it may be that the subject leader role is developed even if the flexible approach is retained and elements of the variety of models is used. With four full-time teachers, the subject leader role is developing in Jane's school through the allocation of specific subject leadership to all staff, who are supported by the headteacher acting as overall subject coordinator.

The headteacher takes the role of the overall subjects coordinator with specific subject leadership being delegated throughout the staff. The implication of this is, that as there are fewer teachers than curriculum areas, teachers carry responsibility for more than one subject area. Therefore, a major part of the role of curriculum leader is to ensure that the programme of curriculum development is planned so no individual member of staff is expected to lead one development area after another. A spread of activity, which is well planned within the school development plan and the staff development programme, ensures that interest and goodwill is retained.

As overall curriculum coordinator I also have responsibility for specific subjects. Having headteacher, teacher and subject responsibilities ensures I am realistic in my expectations from staff as I work to the same guidelines.

The role of curriculum leader is both a challenge and a responsibility. However, I have found that being a headteacher who manages the introduction, delivery and evaluation of the curriculum, is an advantage. The overall view I develop by managing the curriculum throughout the key stages means I can speak with confidence and authority. An unexpected bonus has been the respect for this expertise, which is given by staff as they see the headteacher as a curriculum coordinator who understands the different educational requirements throughout the school.

There are many aspects and expectations within the job description of the curriculum coordinator as shown in the following list:
- lead termly review sessions;
- oversee curriculum planning;
- lead staff development;
- arrange for staff to have equal access to development opportunities;

- be aware of the professional needs of staff;
- oversee the delivery of the subject in the school;
- report to the governors on subject development;
- arrange for subject leaders to inform governors about their subject;
- lead curriculum evenings and in-service training;
- advise, support and guide staff who have individual responsibility for training sessions;
- ensure the policy publication continues to be developed;
- investigate opportunities which will raise staff awareness about curriculum developments;
- involve the school in curriculum initiatives both national and local; and
- monitor the curriculum within school.

I consider one of my most important functions as overall subject coordinator is to meet individual members of staff in the summer term to discuss the achievements, concerns and current situation regarding their subject leadership. This also includes how they aim to develop the subject the next year and what they will require in terms of support etc. It gives an opportunity to acknowledge what has been achieved and how the subject leader contributed to the success.

Over the past years the distribution of subject leadership has been altered. As there are so few opportunities for subject leaders to monitor their subjects within classes, for some subjects, especially the core subjects, we now have a key stage coordinator who works with the subject leader to develop the subject.

Job description

Subject leaders will need your support if their role is to be effective. The question of non-contact time is for each school to judge as to whether it can be afforded. It may be possible to arrange for some joint teaching, giving one-off non-contact time, whilst the leader is working on a specific task or when students are on teaching practice. The subject leader can be supported in other ways:

- being given a clear subject leader job description;
- decisions on fund allocation being decided when the review timetable is drawn up;
- setting up subject leader files for the school which follow the same format;

- being provided with formats for carrying out audits and reviews;
- being given guidance in preparation for inspection;
- receiving in-service for subject knowledge and management skills; and
- the work is timetabled so it is manageable.

The job description should complement the general job description from the conditions of service for teachers and the job specification for the particular employment, including the subjects to be led. You could use a general subject leader job description for all staff with extra specifications to make it relevant for each specific subject. An example developed by one school is included below.

Generic job description

Job title — Subject Leader

Reports to — Headteacher

Responsible for
1　Leading the staff reviews for the subject according to the timings of the development plan and to ensure that documentation is kept up to date.
2　Manage development plan targets which result from school reviews and inspections.
3　Develop targets through liaison with the staff.
4　To prepare responses to other agencies, including governors, as and when required.
5　To make presentations to a variety of groups as and when this is desirable.
6　Maintain a subject file which can be passed to another teacher in case of staff changes or changes in responsibilities.
7　To suggest INSET needs and help in devising ideas for INSET delivery.
8　To audit the subject when this is required, especially when first taking the responsibility.
9　To maintain a resources schedule.
10　To monitor the use of resources and suggest ideas for resource development.
11　To devise a development programme which is consistent with the development plan and make contributions to it as appropriate but which may be for personnel development only.
12　To be active in INSET to develop subject knowledge and management skills.

Review
This description should be reviewed at the time of appraisal.

A subject leader file is one way of keeping documents in an easily retrievable system and will help the leader to be organised. It also makes it simpler to provide evidence during inspection. Ring binders which are colour coded in National

Curriculum colours will make each file immediately recognisable. The suggested headings within each file are:

■ subject policy and schemes;
■ examples of assessed work including photographs;
■ audit and review information;
■ policy review questions;
■ subject development plan;
■ school resources;
■ in-service records and evaluation; and
■ correspondence and resource information.

Providing school formats for a subject audit and ideas for development and resources within the school will help guide the leader as to what is expected and develops a recognised system which everyone can use efficiently. An example of one school's subject leader's audit sheet is included on p. 50:

Management skills can be developed through in-service courses. These will be useful to the present school and if the teacher gains promotion. Management skills include:

■ leading staff during in-service;
■ observation of lessons;
■ monitoring other than by observation;
■ devising subject development plans; and
■ providing subject knowledge.

Schools wishing to develop these skills need to encourage all teachers to understand the aims of management: developing a shared language for subject management will be useful. Remember that the development of the role of the subject leader lends itself to being a school development target in its own right as it will take time and resources.

Summary

■ Decide on the style of curriculum leadership for the school.
■ Be flexible, changing the role and style with changing circumstances.
■ Subject leaders require support to develop the role and the subject.

Each book in *The Subject Leader's Handbook Series* has a chapter on the role of the subject leader.

Subject manager audit

Subject _____ Audit Date _____

Name _____ Date you became this subject manager _____

Subject policy statement exists? _____ Date of last review? _____

Own familiarity with the policy statement _____

_____

Scheme of work exists? _____

Scheme type (e.g. summary, blocked allocation) _____

Own familiarity with the scheme? _____

_____

Notes

1   My ambition for the subject:

_____

_____

2   What I need to find out:

_____

_____

3   What the school and staff could do to help:

_____

_____

4   What I need to do next:

_____

_____

Part three Policy and planning

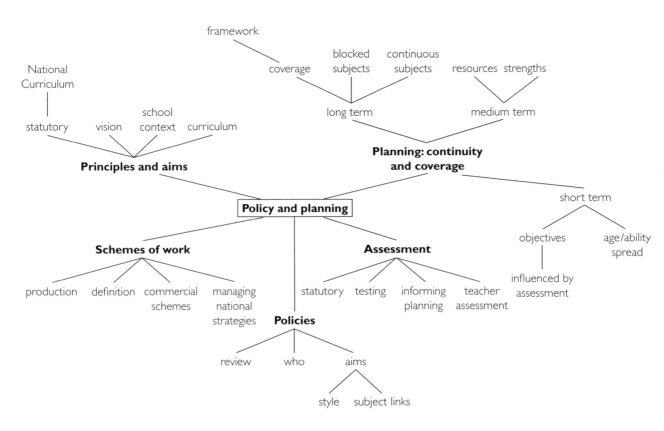

framework

coverage

blocked
subjects

continuous
subjects

resources strengths

National
Curriculum

school
context

statutory   vision   curriculum

long term

medium term

Principles and aims

**Planning: continuity
and coverage**

Policy and planning

short term

objectives

age/ability
spread

Schemes of work

Assessment

influenced by
assessment

production   definition   commercial
schemes

managing
national
strategies

statutory   testing   informing
planning

teacher
assessment

Policies

review   who   aims

style   subject links

Chapter 6

Principles and aims

Aims

Schools working independently and with a variety of starting points often end up with a similar set of aims for the curriculum:

- To provide a broad and balanced curriculum which meets the needs of all pupils.
- To provide equality of opportunity and provision.
- To provide an appropriate curriculum for the different levels of ability.
- To ensure that parents and governors have opportunities to increase their understanding of the curriculum.

These aims are powerful if they are the shared values of the staff, parents, governors and children — as can be seen in Jane's experiences:

> Our starting point was the ethos and standards which, although not recorded, were understood and implemented by all teaching and non-teaching staff, governors and parents. The school was well regarded for the quality of education it delivered and the behaviour of pupils. The staff and governing body then worked together to establish what happened in our school and how we set out to achieve it. The headteacher and governors attended county training on the writing of school aims and objectives and brought this knowledge back to school. Each word and aim was carefully considered and only accepted and recorded when agreement was reached.

Within the written statement the curriculum aims were addressed. Both staff and governors used their knowledge of the school and understanding of children to decide upon the curriculum environment they wished to provide. County advice and support was and still is very useful and the curriculum aim which is published in the school brochure states that our main aim is:

> *To provide a balanced and broadly based curriculum which is relevant to the needs of all children and which will promote the spiritual, moral, cultural, mental and physical development of the children whilst preparing them for the opportunities, experiences and responsibilities of adult life.*

As staff and governors we understand that the aims and objectives are the solid foundation on which we build. Therefore, the aims and objectives, which we agreed, belong to us and we ensure that the parents are aware of them by publishing them in school newsletters, the brochure and by displaying them in school. These are the standards against which we are judged and to which we, as staff and governors, regularly refer. An important exercise has been to review them annually and, to date, only minor alterations have been made.

To maintain the strength of the aims, set up a procedure for reviewing them which involves the relevant personnel. Where numbers are small this process is likely to be quite informal, but keep it pacy by keeping of notes which summarise agreements.

Mission statement

A list of aims themselves will be of less value if they are not set in a broader picture of the vision and intended direction the school is to develop. This is clearly noted by Mel whose school began with a structure to set the aims in the widest possible context.

Most schools produce a mission statement of some kind and a list of aims for the school. These statements are fairly straightforward to draft and most schools proudly display them in their handbook or prospectus. I felt, however, that the challenge for our school was not only to frame our school ethos and intent but to ensure those aims were reflected in all aspects of school policy.

A typical model for meetings when aims are being reviewed is:
- discuss the subject allowing everyone to contribute;
- summarise the points made;
- record agreement; and
- change roles.

Our aims and principles were based within a framework for the curriculum organised under the following headings into which policies are fitted:

- statements of the school ethos and intent;
- detailed statement of whole school aims;
- attitudes, values and monitoring;
- curriculum policies; and
- planning.

Each item in the framework is dependent on the item above it, with the most important, the school ethos and intent, placed at the top.

During this active development, the school's general aims, including mission statements, should be informing the work. Indeed if this phase has not been strongly developed, it will need to be established before beginning the development of more detailed curriculum aims. In this way the approaches to staff levels and resources will be consistent with the overall aims and the ethos of the school will be verbalised and recorded as is the situation in the case study schools whose Mission Statements follow:

Jane's school

At school we work to provide a stimulating and interesting environment, encouraging children to ask questions and develop enquiring and creative minds. We endeavour to establish a trusting relationship between children and staff, trying wherever possible to make school an extension of home and community.

Mel's school

Our school is committed to providing the highest quality of education for all our children, which nourishes their diverse talents within the context of a positive and caring family atmosphere.

Managing the curriculum within set principles

Schools also have to ensure they meet the statutory requirements of the National Curriculum. As this evolves nationally, it should also be evolved within your school, with a clear development plan to show that the process is under way. Surveys of the National Curriculum in rural authorities with many smaller schools, showed that the delivery of the curriculum was as effective as in larger schools. This is largely because all schools viewed the National Curriculum as a vehicle for implementing a structured curriculum which has continuity and progression at its core. It provides the reason and purpose for curriculum development so is a positive tool for the curriculum manager. Even with national schemes of work, small schools will need to plan a realistic period of adapting them to their circumstances.

The influence of the school's beliefs and its ethos should be able to be traced through to the actual delivery of the curriculum. It is an interesting exercise to trace back actual activities to see if they are consistent, but it is more useful to be aware of the hierarchy of interacting levels as curriculum aims develop. In this way the general statements of intent will be meaningful rather than hollow wishes and dreams, and will ensure that the school has a purposeful and clear vision.

The following illustrates how Mel showed an awareness of the hierarchy and ensured a consistent approach to the management of the curriculum within set principles which establish clear aims for everyone working within the school. It is summarised in the following framework:

Mel's school — Framework for the curriculum

Statement of the school ethos and intent

Detailed statement of whole school aims

Attitudes, values and monitoring

teaching and learning	quality and expectations	assessment	recording and reporting	SEN
pupil self-esteem	responding to children's work	pastoral	role in the community	equal opportunities

Curriculum policies

		English	maths	science				
history	geography	D & T	IT	art	music	PE	RE	

Long-term planning
2 or 4 yearly cycle ensuring coverage of the NC by the whole school and time allocation to each subject area

Medium-term planning
Termly detailed plan of work showing: points of focus, key learning objectives and
approaches undertaken in each key stage including resources and assessment opportunities

Short-term planning
Weekly notes made by the teacher of specific classroom planning

The school's framework for the curriculum helped us to identify the purpose and aspirations of the school. It has allowed us to focus our thinking on the key areas of attitudes, values and monitoring before beginning the adoption of policy statements for individual subject areas.

The order in which we tackled each area of the framework was very important as we needed to get the system up and running as quickly as possible. The statement of the school ethos and intent was our natural starting point. We had to make decisions about what our school was all about. This involved considerable staff discussion as we sought to identify the essence of the school's aspirations and then set these ideas into the short mission statement. This statement was presented to the governors alongside the planned framework for the curriculum. In our particular case, the statement of intent focused on the close, caring relationships that can be developed in a very small school. The small numbers of children involved in the school community allowed children to: develop as individuals, consider the needs of others and receive close attention from the teachers.

A recorded list of aims produced by our case-study schools may form a useful starting point for those within your school, or help you review those already established. The list produced for the purposes of this book is included to show how the process of developing them can be concluded rather than trying to be a complete illustration. Developing and reviewing is a management tool for the school to use to ensure an agreed set of beliefs and is more effective than just adopting a prepared list. Everyone involved in this work will be aware of the recorded results in all their possible formats.

Mel's school — Whole school aims

- To provide a sound education that will nourish the diverse talents of our children.
- To provide a happy, caring, secure and stimulating environment.
- To develop a thirst for knowledge and a desire to learn.
- To create a sense of wonder, enjoyment and enthusiasm.
- To enable each child to realise their potential through high expectations and challenging tasks.
- To allow all children equal opportunities and access to an entitlement curriculum.
- To widen the children's horizons to enable them to live life to the full.
- To help the children to develop values that will guide them through the difficult decisions they will, inevitably, have to make in adult life.
- To encourage children to become responsible, self-confident and self-motivated.
- To develop qualities of respect, consideration and tolerance for others.
- To value every member of the school community, nurture self-esteem and encourage caring and good humoured relationships.
- To create an atmosphere of partnership in education between children, teachers and parents.
- To maintain strong links with the local community.
- To offer a curriculum which is 'balanced and broadly based' which 'promotes the spiritual, moral, cultural, mental and physical development' of the pupils in our care, and which will begin 'to prepare them for the opportunities, responsibilities and experiences of adult life'.

Children can be involved in developing the list, which can then be interpreted as positive behaviour statements for both children and staff. The format could be in the form of a code which includes how to be a good class member or a good friend, a playtime code etc. and published as guide sheets or included in a class book which is reviewed and read during circle times or class assembly. Contributions can be made through drawings by children showing cooperative behaviour. The format and language will need to be adapted to suit the age and maturity of the children. Again this type of work is more powerful when they have been involved in its development.

Summary

- Curriculum aims are set in the context of the general aims and vision of the school.
- Aims are most effective when developed and reviewed as a shared process.

Chapter 7

Planning the curriculum: continuity and coverage

When planning for continuity and coverage small schools may have particular features which influence them, including:

■ more than one age group per class;

■ classes which cross the key stages;

■ split age groups in different classes.

A programme of work based on a three-year cycle in Key Stage 1 and a four-year cycle in Key Stage 2 may be possible; or perhaps a two-year cycle for each class. The Literacy Strategy, for example, has been planned on a two-year cycle to help schools which have two year groups in each class. Schools with even more year groups per class will be dependent on differentiating through group and individual work or by adopting a ninety-minute strategy. This includes half an hour of other work to allow for two periods of 'whole class' work. In all this planning, the use of support staff and voluntary help may be an important small school requirement.

Another challenge may be caused by the need to restructure due to a change in numbers or because of a varied number of children in each year group.

In every case it is important not to let what SCAA described as 'blocked work' dominate the planning. The more important continuous work of developing concepts, skills and attitudes in the programmes for English, maths and investigational

Each book in *The Subject Leader's Handbook Series* has a section on planning the curriculum.

science should lead the planning. Blocked work such as the history study units of Key Stage 2 may be more suitably planned as a separate unit of work so that cohorts can be tracked through them. An alternative could be to adjust the planning for a specific group who may experience the work as a 'lighter touch'. A scheme of work that emphasises skills, concepts and attitudes should lessen the impact of having to allow children to cover specific content in different ways, whilst the level descriptors can be used to plan for differentiation.

Long-term planning

Coverage of the Programmes of Study should be ensured at the long-term level of planning. This level of planning is increasingly being provided to schools such as the literacy and numeracy developments, and the schemes of work for other subjects. For small schools an important balance needs to be maintained between frameworking content and the flexibility allowing for changing circumstances. Foundation subjects especially may need even more careful long-term planning due to the curriculum streamlining. Long-term planning has been undertaken within our study schools:

Jane:

The planning in the school has progressed from a topic style which was centred around the science curriculum with the remaining curriculum being adapted to fit, and in some cases contrived to fit, to the current system of a three-year cycle for Key Stage 1, and two two-year cycles for Key Stage 2. The Key Stage 2 cycle is based on a class for Years 3 and 4 and another for Years 5 and 6. This detailed planning document is taking longer to record than was first envisaged because we have recently moved from being a three-class school to a four-class school. Initial work has had to be revised and re-arranged within long-term plans. However, the advantage of the method of planning we have adopted is that it does allow flexibility of approach which is necessary for a smaller school as class organisation frequently alters from year to year. Therefore, the arrangement of the curriculum described below is not a perfect model but has proved to be an effective starting point.

The previous method of recording planning had been for each teacher to plan on a half or term basis and to keep a tick sheet record of work which was then passed on to the next teacher. We were in agreement that this system was not efficient with concerns being expressed that there could be gaps in delivery and certain areas of the curriculum would not be properly addressed. Staff development sessions were planned which would allow us time to begin this major project. Our target was to develop a system of long-term planning which would identify the termly coverage of Programmes of Study before each subject. We had an excellent starting point in this work as the advisory section for the authority were running training courses on the subject of long-term planning. I attended one of the courses and returned to school with sufficient knowledge to lead staff in the development of planning.

A decision was made to begin with the science curriculum, as this was the area in which confidence was greatest. Using our local authority building blocks method we started with Key Stage 1 and composed a three-year chart with the autumn, spring, and summer terms clearly marked for years A, B and C, see example below. We proceeded to identify within each term an area of the science curriculum; this ensured that at the end of the three years the child who had started in our reception class had covered all the Programmes of Study for Key Stage 1 science. Throughout the process we tracked the child, referring back to National Curriculum documents.

Autumn
Year A — Light
sources — that light comes from a variety of sources including the sun, that darkness is the absence of light
Year B — Plants
growth and reproduction groups
Year C — Humans
similarities and differences, the body, life cycles, senses

Spring
Year A — Changing materials
effects of forces, effects of heat
Year B — Sound
sources — hearing, circuit
Year C — Forces
motion, shaping

Summer
Year A — Properties of materials
          similarities and differences
Year B — Health
          food, medicine
Year C — Similarities and differences
          habitats

By following this format we could ensure that during Key Stage 1 each child met the Programmes of Study once in depth at the appropriate level. The level of depth has been a significant factor and staff feel this planning arrangement allows them to allocate sufficient time to each Programme of Study and offers opportunities to assess pupils. Previous planning arrangements had afforded an inbalance of time allocated with limited opportunities for assessment.

Having learned a method of approach with which the staff was comfortable we proceeded to Key Stage 2. A two-year cycle was allocated to Years 3 and 4 and 5 and 6. The science Programmes of Study were allocated once throughout each two-year cycle therefore ensuring that within Key Stage 2 pupils met the Programmes of Study twice at progressive levels. By the end of this exercise the staff felt confident that the science curriculum had proper coverage and continuity.

We then followed the same process with the remaining areas of the curriculum. Staff worked in key stage pairs to apportion the curriculum ensuring that throughout the key stages pupils met all Programmes of Study and that links were made when possible but were not contrived. Within an academic year pupils will have two terms when geography is taught and two when history is taught. By allowing a term when one is not taught more time is released to study a subject such as the Romans in more depth.

For some areas of the curriculum it was decided that the subject leader would assign the Programmes of Study. This had a two-fold benefit. Firstly it ensured the subject leader was familiar with the progression of their subject, and secondly, staff who had less expertise in this area felt confident that pupils would receive a curriculum appropriate to their needs.

Work on long-term planning is an on-going process planned with the school development plan. Information technology has been identified as an area for development through policy and skills progression. During the time this method has been in use some of the principle benefits have been staff security in the knowledge that all pupils meet all Programmes of Study. Each teacher has clear guidance in the curriculum they must teach and all staff have knowledge about the progression of the curriculum in school. Any member of staff, permanent or temporary, can at a glance be informed of the curriculum being taught and governors have improved their familiarity with the curriculum as it is easier to discuss progress when the planning is clearly laid out in this form.

Mel:

It was particularly important to put in place a rigid long-term plan of curriculum coverage to meet the challenge presented by the fact that children remain in the same class with the same teacher for an entire key stage. It was impossible to simply designate specific themes to year groups. Year 3 would not always be the time children would be taught about the Vikings, for example. Curriculum coverage had to be spread over a number of years.

A four-year programme indicating the content of the curriculum and placing each area of study into a time slot appeared to be the best solution to ensure coverage of all aspects of the National Curriculum.

We had to be able to look at the National Curriculum and identify where children would meet each programme and establish a spiral system of challenges according to the age of the children. Many crucial decisions had to be made, including, for example, which themes from history and geography to cover, as we laid out the National Curriculum on planning sheets. The governing principle was to keep the curriculum manageable and avoid overloading of the system by attempting to achieve too much in each term. It would have been very easy to be unrealistic in our expectations.

The programme gives a framework, shown below, for each term of each year upon which medium-term planning is then based. The Key Stage 1 programme is a two-year cycle while the Key Stage 2 programme is a four-year model.

Areas of continuous work and areas of blocked work form units of identified work. Wherever possible, links were sought between matching curriculum areas, for example:
- rivers in geography with load bearing structures in design technology;

- ancient Egypt in history with Moses in religious education;
- models with lights in design technology with electricity in science; and
- textiles in art with textiles design in design technology and materials in science.

Linking themes in this way has helped children recognise the relationships between different areas of knowledge, providing that the strong focus of interest as a broad theme is followed during the term — as the example which follows shows. It has enabled us, as teachers, to reduce the work load of the curriculum into manageable proportions.

Some subject areas, such as maths and English, follow a broad yearly cycle ensuring, for example, all children encounter the theme of capacity in maths at least once a year. Other areas, including science and geography, follow a two-yearly cycle, while subjects like history and religious education at Key Stage 2 follow a four-yearly pattern. In this way every child will visit each area of the science curriculum three times during their primary school career, at Key Stage 1; in Years 3 or 4; and in Years 5 or 6. Key Stage 2 children will meet history themes such as the Tudors only once.

Percentages of teaching time were allocated to each subject on a yearly basis in order to achieve a balance across the curriculum and were used to inform medium-term planning. For instance, one term may be heavily biased towards history whereas the following term may contain little emphasis on the subject. However, over the course of the year the overall balance of time will be what we consider to be desirable. It was also decided to place greater emphasis on certain areas at Key Stage 1 such as English, music and personal and social education; and at Key Stage 2 sport, drama, music and personal and social education.

Formats for the recording of the planning will vary according to the subject and the interpretations of your school. You could use a framework of study units over the teaching cycle where the subject is easily blocked according to content. History is a typical example, but elements of geography, science, music, religious education, technology, information technology and art may also be readily blocked by content. Another method is to show when programmes will be taught by pasting a sheet next to them. This sheet is then divided to provide spaces for

Mel's school — Framework for long-term planning KS 2

	English	Maths	Science	DT	IT	PE	RE	Music	History	Geography	Art	Other Seasonal
Term 1	English work will be 'ongoing' covering all aspects of the NC Areas have been 'blocked in' to illustrate main focus points; revise planning and drafting skills; report and factual writing; drama	Maths work will be 'ongoing' covering all aspects of the NC Areas have been 'blocked in' to illustrate main focus points; place value; length; angles and direction (at least two investigations)	people, circulation, organs, skeletons; types of material (classifying and examining properties)	textiles (Designing and making: Y3/4 belt bags Y5/6 slippers)	IT will be incorporated across the curriculum main Areas have been 'blocked in' to illustrate main focus points; word processing; control	The village hall will be used throughout the term on one afternoon each week to allow: gymnastics, dance, country dancing (One weekly outdoor games period to cover:) rugby, shinty, football, handball games	church life aspects of Christianity methodism baptists RC etc.		Romans, Anglo Saxons, Vikings		textiles (sewing) lettering; techniques and layout	harvest (food and farming)
Term 2	Narrative writing — techniques for story planning; book writing for younger audience	shape; probability; money; capacity; area (at least two investigations)	light; sound	Y5/6 (Sheet materials) Y3/4 book making	DTP; Compose	(Two weekly outdoor games periods to cover:) rugby, shinty, football	stories from the old testament (women in the bible); Lent		Ancient Greece	settlements (minor)	collage; art in the past and present; studying an important artist's work (Picasso); sculpting	Making your own decisions; production; Easter
Term 3	Speaking and listening — (presentation skills); non-fiction reading, research and note taking; persuasive writing	data handling; computation; time; fractions; weight (at least two investigations)	forces; living (nutrition, fitness, health ed, sex ed, drug awareness, safety)	Frame-work materials: Vehicle making	data handling; drawing programs	Swimming (Two weekly outdoor games periods to cover:) cricket, rounders; athletics; outdoor challenges	Sikhism; Jesus (the man who changed lives); history of Christianity			India, Chembacoli (pack) (contrasting place)	drawing techniques; art in other cultures	the body; SATs; church school's festival; sports day

Spanning items:

- DT (across all terms): food; construction sets
- Music (across all terms): recorders; music in assembly — composers + performers, old + new, different cultures listening and appreciating (detailed follow up once a term); hymn practice; pitch, dynamics etc, p.106; place (Indian music)
- Geography (across all terms): weather recording (minor)

Top grouping headers: Key Stage 2 (History, Geography, Art); Year 2 (Other Seasonal)

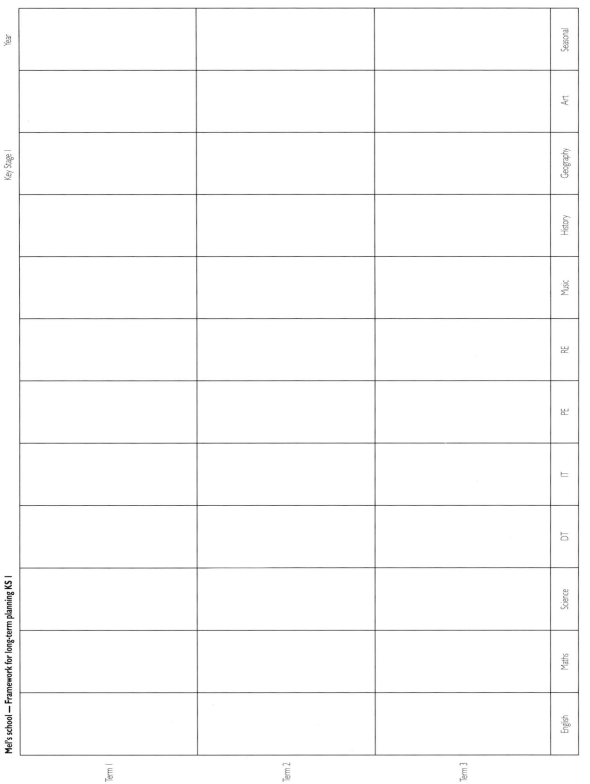

Mel's school — Framework for long-term planning KS 1

	English	Maths	Science	DT	IT	PE	RE	Music	History	Geography	Art	Seasonal
Term 1												Year
Term 2												Key Stage 1
Term 3												

each class and may show that programmes will be visited a number of times by the children. In cases where an age group has had to be split, this method will show whether they still cover all programmes even if in a slightly different context.

Schemes of work which allow for children's varying development will be more suitable for the continuous type of Programmes of Study, such as in English and mathematics. They are more like threads, which are available according to present levels even though the content is introduced to a group or class. This will allow for the differentiation of the curriculum and take into account the multi-age groups within small school classes. This type of long-term planning involves planning a hierarchy of skills as in, for example, geography skills and investigative science. You could use published materials as a starting point for developing these schemes, but most schools have also developed their own totally independently to reflect their particular circumstances. The starting point for the skill structure should be developed by analysing those included in the Programmes of Study of the National Curriculum.

This system of planning has similarities for teachers in every primary school, although introducing a topic to many age groups may be less successful in a small school.

Summary

- Blocked Programmes of Study are allocated to classes or teaching years.
- Continuous Programmes of Study are devised as schemes of work.
- An element of flexibility needs to be retained for changing circumstances.
- Formats may vary for each school and for different subjects.
- Blocked content should not be allowed to dominate the planning cycle.

Medium-term planning

Medium-term plans should be reasonably brief explanations of how the long-term plans are put into action for each term or module of work, such as the work for half a term of the Literacy Hour.

Some teachers may use a grid format representing each week of a term to plan out the allocated curriculum (see p. 70). This can be used to keep the pace of the work going even though built-in spaces will be required to help expand work or take special events into account. A grid can help with forward preparation of resources and structure the work to give an even distribution on the time demands for the teacher.

There also needs to be a format for linking the actual Programmes of Study to the class work and to provide spaces to evaluate the work (see p. 71).

Devising a successful approach to this level of planning is a challenging task, but has many rewards. The breadth and depth of a curriculum is easily demonstrated to all the staff and any external agencies. Governors can be a party to the plans, so have an appropriate level of knowledge and feel secure that the school is meeting the statutory requirements of the curriculum. In larger primary schools, which have developed the role of the curriculum leader, medium-term plans can be discussed to help with subject knowledge; they can also be collected to provide a clear picture of how a subject is taught throughout the school. For example, if advice is sought from advisory teachers or LEA officers, medium-term plans can be an appropriate starting point. This advice may also be in the form of subject knowledge or successful teaching strategies and useful resources.

Surveying the resources required at this level of planning is often very successful, as it ensures that resources can be purchased in the quantities required — it is an effective use of limited finances. When teaching electrical circuits, for example, it is disheartening to discover that batteries or bulbs are no longer in stock. Medium-term plans also can be used to plan for the sharing of resources, again making the best use of them within the school. Time is also used more effectively in the preparation of resources. As the planning cycle develops, the resources are also developed, allowing for a distribution of finance to be made according to where the need is greatest.

Charlie's school — Medium-term planning forecast sheet

Week	1	2	3	4	5	6	7
English							
Mathematics							
Science							
IT							
Technology							
History							
Geography							
Music							
Art							
PE							
RE							

© Falmer Press

Charlie's school
Medium-term planning sheet

Class
Subject .... Term .... Topic ....
Teacher ....

Areas of experience	Skills	Learning aims	Activities	PoS DLO	Evaluation

In any size of school, medium-term plans can be used for successful liaison:

■ between staff who share a class — for example, where there is a teaching headteacher;

■ between staff who share an age group to ensure appropriate coverage of the curriculum for all children, giving equal opportunities of access;

■ by the subject leader; and

■ by staff liaising within and between key stages to ensure continuity and progression.

Medium-term plans can also be used for monitoring, particularly by the teaching headteacher who often will find it more difficult to monitor short-term plans. In small schools this can be carried out at staff meetings when everyone shares their planning. These meetings are usually successful as they contribute to an open management style often adopted in small schools, and help to foster good working relationships by showing that everyone is working in a focused way. Ideas for planning and preparing tasks for children may be shared incidentally at this type of meeting, so that good practice is not hidden in just one part of the school.

The experiences of Mel and Jane continue to illustrate the possible styles and approaches that can be used in small schools.

Jane:

The second strand of planning is the medium-term planning which is a more detailed recording of the learning that takes place over the term and is directly linked to the long-term planning cycle. Each subject is planned for on a separate form. The planning is recorded under:

> subject title; the Programmes of Study which will be covered; learning objectives appropriate to the different levels in the class; resources which will be used; the skills which will be learned and some examples of differentiated activities which will be employed.

This method of planning has been effective in that it focuses the mind of the teacher on the work to be covered and clearly identifies the need to provide for the different levels of ability. When a mixed key stage class was a feature of the school, the teacher completed subject planning forms for each key stage thereby ensuring that the pupils were taught at an appropriate level.

Staff have recognised that a major advantage of this method of planning, which identifies the need to be aware of the Programmes of Study for subjects and the learning objectives for different levels, brings an increased understanding and familiarity with the National Curriculum documents. This improved knowledge has led to gaps in delivery being identified and subsequently planned for, an example being the provision for investigative maths. A second advantage is that by using identified differentiated learning objectives, planning for assessment is simplified and becomes part of the planning process.

The use of our forms continues to be an area for staff discussion as we continually, as all schools do, try to seek a means of recording skills progression which is not a tick sheet of acquisition nor a necessity to write progress of recorded achievements. However, we are happier with this format than others we have trialled and each medium-term planning sheet has proved to be an excellent document for headteacher meetings with individual staff to discuss their planning for the next term. Throughout the term they are a ready reference for teachers and the headteacher, and because they are at the end of each term they have already been found to be extremely useful as we repeat the cycle.

Mel:

Once the long-term curriculum plan was agreed, an in-service session near the end of each term was devoted to the joint planning of the delivery of the following term's curriculum. This is our medium-term planning. As an alternative to using designated INSET days for planning we have often employed two supply teachers for a day to release both staff to carry out the joint planning. We felt it was important to invest quality time into the planning process away from the classroom and not squeeze it into a staff meeting at the end of a full day of teaching.

Careful medium-term planning has been responsible for a more focused approach to teaching. Removing the clutter of a crowded curriculum and identifying the precise knowledge and skills to be taught and assessed during a term makes for a more manageable curriculum. As a classroom teacher you know exactly what you are aiming to achieve and how you will judge your success. Distilling the curriculum down to realistic and manageable components in this way leaves the teacher secure and confident they are covering the curriculum thoroughly while leaving them room to occasionally pursue the important spontaneous lesson which fires the children's imagination and presents itself when the school bus breaks down, for example, or when a frog is discovered in a lunch box.

In a two-teacher school it is possible to take a comprehensive look at the delivery of the curriculum throughout the school. The joint planning sessions have enabled teachers to gain an overview of the whole school in terms of progression and continuity. The sessions also provide the opportunity to raise levels of educational thinking and for curriculum-based staff development by placing discussion of curriculum issues in a real and relevant context.

Each medium-term planning session begins with an evaluation of the previous term's teaching. This is an opportunity to reflect on many aspects of teaching and learning including successes, organisation, standards of attainment and things to amend when next teaching that particular area.

Subjects are considered in turn and a programme of work designed to meet the desirable learning outcomes. Together we consider the learning objectives presented by a particular subject throughout the school and what we would expect from the youngest children and the oldest children in the school. By referring to school policies and the National Curriculum documents we lay out a spectrum of learning for the whole school then divide it into units for each age

Mel's school — Medium-term planning

Class .... Theme/Subject .... Academic Year ....

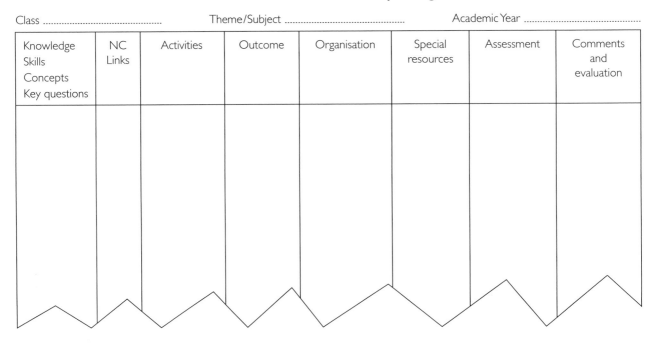

Knowledge Skills Concepts Key questions	NC Links	Activities	Outcome	Organisation	Special resources	Assessment	Comments and evaluation

group. For example, in science when planning a whole school theme of sound we identified the key concepts we felt children should learn. These ended up being broadly the same regardless of age range — namely, how sound travels, pitch and amplification. Three programmes of work were then designed for Key Stage 1; Years 3 and 4; and Years 5 and 6. Each programme complemented the others and varied in its degree of challenge and depth of knowledge according to the age of the children.

This programme was set out on a matrix which allowed us to highlight the concept we wished to introduce; links with other curriculum areas; activities we had planned; expected outcomes; organisation planning; special resources needed; and opportunities for assessment. The final comments and evaluation column would be completed at the end of the term (see above).

The matrix is completed horizontally as each activity is planned. We decided not to refer to specific coding of any kind on our grid as we felt these would be subject to change and can be confusing. Once the matrix is completed a glance down the organisation column, for example, can reveal the balance and variety of the approaches to be employed by the teacher — a combination of group work, individual and whole class teaching opportunities.

Mel's school
Age: Yr 3/4

Theme/subject — Science: sound

Academic year: Spring '97

Knowledge Skills Concepts Key questions	NC links	Activities	Outcome	Organisation	Special resources	Assessment	Comments and evaluation
Vibration		Tuning fork and water dish (p. 5 experiment 'sound pack' notes 6)	i) sound is carried by vibration ii) sound travels through air in waves	Whole group (Display of musical instruments)	'Sound Pack' (instrument collection)		
Pitch	Music	i) Demonstration on guitar ii) Make bridged instrument and move bridge (pp. 5–6 experiment 5)	i) difference between high and low notes ii) the length and thickness of string affects pitch iii) a shorter string gives a higher note	pairs using equipment from sound pack		Can identify high/low notes. Transfer ideas to observation of guitar playing	
Vibrating air — reeds	Music	Make a hooter from straws: use a funnel to amplify the sound — compare to woodwind instruments	i) vibrating air makes a sound ii) shorter columns of air make higher notes iii) a 'bell' on the end amplifies the sound	individual / whole class / write up report in science book	Art straws / Selection of woodwind instruments	Children each make a 'hooter' then organise the group into order according to pitch — highest to lowest	
Amplification — loudness	Music	Compare difference between using sound box and just the lid (experiment 10)	A hollow chamber amplifies sound — compare to guitar/violin	pairs	Sound pack	Ask children to make the loudest/quietest sound they can from their equipment	
Sound travels through different materials		Put ear to desk top — drum fingers, place ticking watch on forehead etc. (refer to science books)	Sound can travel through other things as well as air e.g. can hear plane overhead through glass (no sound in vacuum/outer space — discuss)	class discussion			
		Make string telephone (experiment 14)	String must be tight for vibration to travel and carry sound	pairs	Sound pack, plastic pots, string	Are messages transferred?	

Examining the special resources column can identify resources to be purchased before the start of the next term (see p. 75).

For many subjects the matrix is completed for a whole key stage and identifies a range of activities and expected outcomes according to the age and abilities of the children in the class. This is particularly important in areas such as history, religious education, physical education and geography where one theme will be followed by a whole key stage in one classroom but at varying levels of challenge.

The medium-term plan should be used as a device to ensure all the relevant aspects of the curriculum are covered but, through careful pruning of what is not absolutely necessary, leave freedom and time for teachers to follow the occasional bouts of spontaneity which keep teaching alive and fulfilling. Above all long- and medium-term planning does work! It defines exact areas of coverage and that makes the teacher's job of mapping out the daily diet of work so much quicker and easier. The planning matrix has helped us remain focused on the purpose and expectations of each lesson and ensures we still remain loyal to the principles set out in our teaching and learning policy.

Short-term planning

Short-term planning refers to single lesson plans or linked groups of lessons. They are involved with more specific teaching objectives, which contribute to the broader statements in the National Curriculum documents. They could include the different expectations for children and assessment opportunities when this is appropriate.

There are a wide variety of approaches to record planning at this level. Some schools use a weekly diary, others have specific formats allowing the recording of the objectives being taught which contribute to the aims of the medium-term plans. The style chosen should complement the formats of the medium-term plans so repetition is avoided. For example, if Programmes of Study are referred to by their National Curriculum code on the medium-term plans these need not be recorded on the short-term planning.

Alongside the style of the planning there are other issues for smaller schools especially as they involve age ranges within each class as well as the use of short-term planning to monitor the curriculum as indicated by Jane:

> The third strand of the planning structure is short-term planning which takes the form of a weekly forecast of work to be completed, plus space for a review of the week and opportunities to be used for assessment. The short-term planning identifies in more depth the different activities, which will be used to achieve the learning objectives. It is directly related to the medium-term planning. As a staff we agreed that I, as headteacher, will read the short-term planning each week and this has proved to be an excellent means of ensuring that I know what is happening in each class and can speak with firm knowledge to parents and governors.

Formats should allow for the variety of the curriculum so that work can be informed by the assessment of the children. For example, when teaching subtraction to a mixed age and ability class some children will be ready to move to the next level whilst others will still require consolidation and continued practice. For lessons which are going to be combined, perhaps over several weeks, a different format may be more appropriate as each lesson will not be informing the planning of the next. Work which is blocked by content may also fall into this category as children may not revisit it, no matter what their level of understanding, following the teaching time allocated to it. Evaluation of this type of work could, however, inform the concept and skill level that will be appropriate when teaching different content — such as the next history study unit, for example.

The different formats for different types of work are illustrated by the following examples which were devised by another school. The first aims to make specific objectives clear and to encourage a pacy style of lesson. There are spaces to record whether children have completed the tasks and achieved the learning objectives. This format is not designed to be used in every lesson, and it can also be used where several lessons are contributing to the learning objective. The second format can be used for blocked units, where individual lessons contribute to the learning objectives identified and assessment will be usually completed at the end of the programme. It can also be used for on-going types of lessons, such as using the

Charlie's school — Planning and assessment systems for Year 5/6

Class	Year Groups — Year 5/6		Date commenced		
Time	Subject	Date of evaluation:	Date completed		
Dates	Activity and organisation	EVALUATION	Assessment — name	F	Acvd	NA

Learning objectives (purpose)	Outline teacher/child time **Exposition**				
Success criteria (assessment evidence)	**Task**				
Organisation: (Class) (Group)	**Differentiation**	**Resources**			
Exposition					
Groupings					
Criteria					
Task					
Context of work					
Next stage of learning (after assessment)					

Charlie's school — Short-term planning

Primary school *Ongoing STP sheet*	Planning and assessment systems		Short-term planning sheet	Year
Class		**Year groups**	**Resources**	
Time		**Subject**		
Learning aims or objective(s) (purpose)	**Task**		**Dates/groups and evaluative notes**	**Differentiation**
				Organisation: (class) (group)
				Exposition
				Groupings
				Criteria
				Task
				Context of work
				Next stage of learning

© Falmer Press

imaginative play area, which are part of the Desirable Learning Outcomes for under-5-year-old children; and for the short mental maths work in both key stages.

Good recording formats are not just for accountability but highlight the positive contribution teachers are making to the teaching and learning which is taking place. Teachers should be encouraged to share any ideas which help them with thorough short-term planning but make it easier to manage in terms of time and the amount of planning generated. Resources, for example, may need only to be recorded as reminders if necessary. Another example is where work is on-going and planned in a similar way, so that one detailed plan serves for many lessons. There may be many lessons of this type such as writing patterns in the early years and

Charlie's school — Activity differentiation sheet
(Optional planning sheet, used when considered to be useful)
NB Use in conjunction with 'Levels of Differentiation' sheet.

Activity: _____

_____

Learning Objectives: _____

_____

All children will:
Most children will:
Some children will:
The most able children will:

handwriting practice in later years. The format above can be used to illustrate the different levels of learning which still occur during on-going lessons of this type.

Mel describes the short-term planning which has been devised within his school:

The short-term curriculum plan is largely a working document for the purposes of the teacher only. On it the teacher sets out the work prepared for the week showing organisation, details of groups, resources etc. and recording areas of focus. The content of lessons is taken directly from the medium-term planning sheets and is informed by the teacher's judgment on how a particular theme or concept is progressing. The teacher uses their professional experience to re-shape or reinforce any part of the medium-term plan to ensure the desired outcome. For instance, if a group of children are not secure in their knowledge of place value to one hundred to the level the teacher thinks they are capable of achieving, additional work may be provided. In the same way, a theme may create such enthusiasm in a class or individual that the teacher feels they wish to allow the children to explore further.

Short-term curriculum planning is also where you deal with the important question of teaching with many age groups in one room.

Mel's school — Weekly planning

Week beginning: _____

	9:15	9:35	10:45	11:00	12:05	1:05		2:45	3:00	3:30
Mon	Whole school assembly		B		L			B		
Tue			R		U	Whole school singing		R		
Wed	Whole school assembly		E		N			E		
Thu	Radio/class assembly		A		C			A		
Fri	Whole school sharing assembly		K		H			K		

Notes

Having been initially fairly terrified at the daunting prospect of handling a variety of age groups combined with different ability levels all at the same time and in the same room I now find it difficult to conceive of any other way of teaching. An established pattern of teaching and learning has been set up with older children supporting younger children when appropriate.

Sometimes a whole class approach can be used: poetry writing from a shared stimulus, for instance, for a whole class starting point, with restrictions placed on certain age or ability groups. For example, if the outcome of a lesson is to retell the story of the first invasion of Britain by the Romans, the whole class could be told the story, watch a video, act it out etc., but when writing a report younger children could produce their own by using a scribe, older children could submit the information with additional facts and arguments discovered in books, CDs etc., and other children could record the story from memory using the support of word banks. The key point from a classroom management point of view is that the teacher is only required to be with one group while the others work independently. Once a teacher has completed the group work it can be copied or put on an OHT for children to use for their own individual recording which allows the teacher time to assess and support the work being carried out by the rest of the class.

Whole class lessons can involve groups of mixed age and ability. For example, which group can make the strongest bridge from two sheets of A4 paper and three paper clips? Another example is a trading activity linked to Ancient Greece where each group lives on a different island with a limited variety of commodities which they must trade with other islands which have a surplus of different items, in order to provide a balance of goods for their people.

The teacher can only be in one place at a time so lessons must be carefully paced to allow maximum teacher time for each group of children at crucial points in the lesson. In a maths lesson, for instance, children may be working in year groups or sometimes double year groups. A trickle system of teacher input can be used to visit each group of pupils at key times in the lesson. The teacher sets off one group with a high level of discussion and teacher time while other groups work more independently — completing tasks, working from books, working from the board etc., which are designed to be completed over different intervals. Once the first group has been set their task after the initial discussion the teacher is able to take each group in turn as they finish their more independent work and then set them new tasks for the lesson. Once everyone is working the teacher can call groups together to give extra help or draw out specific teaching points. This is a very active teaching style but makes the most out of the limited working time.

Personally, I have never found a system of listing work on the board to be covered in the child's own time during the day, or having lots of groups working on many different activities, very efficient. I cannot switch instantly from geography to maths and then to art as I visit different activities. Such lessons can appear to be without a group focus. There is no way of re-capping and summarising what has been learnt at the end of the session and there is a danger that without firm directed control some children, especially those with highly developed avoiding tactics, might never complete anything.

I therefore try to restrict the subjects on the go in classroom at any one time to a maximum of two, apart from computer activities. The teacher then bounces between the two, giving help and instructions to one group as the other reaches a stage when they can work more independently before the next opportunity for teacher input is reached. This works best for equipment-intensive subjects such as art and science where there would not be enough space or equipment to allow more than one group to work at a time.

It is the job of the teacher to teach and lessons must be controlled in a way which allows quality time for that to happen, otherwise the teacher could be reduced to crowd control or a bystander. The approach for each lesson must be assessed separately and a wide variety of approaches used. Time is the essential factor; finding techniques to ensure none is wasted is the challenge.

To cope with all the various work sheets and completed pieces of work generated by the different age groups each year band has a clip file containing clear A4 plastic pockets. As each new piece of work is undertaken a tick sheet stating the title of the piece of work and a list of children in the year group is placed into an empty pocket. As each child finishes they place their completed work in the appropriate pocket and take off their name. This allows you and the children to monitor the production of work.

Parental classroom support has been vital as the delicate balance of pupil numbers and uncertain future roll numbers prevents a small school like ours employing permanent help. However, every parent that does not go to work or have other commitments comes into school on a regular basis to help in the classroom. This helps to organise work which requires small, supervised groups, such as playing the recorder or cooking. It helped us set up a science programme where one teacher takes a Year 5 and Year 6 group, another takes a Year 3 and Year 4 group while the Key Stage 1 group cook with two parents, with the groups changing on the three-weekly system. This reduces group size and allows the teacher to concentrate on a single class lesson and discussion after.

Summary

- Long-term planning sets out the framework for the whole curriculum.
- Medium-term planning shows how the long-term plans will be put into action for each term or module of work.
- Short-term planning is based on learning objectives which can be measured.
- Formats contribute to the quality of teaching and learning and are not simply for accountability.
- A variety of formats may be required.
- Planning includes organisation, tasks and assessment.
- A flexible teaching style should be linked to the objectives.
- Planned voluntary help is the most useful.

Chapter 8   Assessment

See also *Coordinating assessment practice across the primary school* in this series.

Many smaller primary schools have a very clear knowledge about the children's level of achievement due to the smaller numbers and because teachers often have children in their classes for more than one year. There are many types of assessment taking place in schools and the success of an assessment policy and its structure requires clarity of the purpose, regular reviews and the meeting of national requirements.

Teaching children of different year groups whilst others are involved in statutory assessment and testing, is one of the organisational problems often encountered. The counter-balance is that the small number of children may make the Key Stage 1 SATs more manageable. Effective strategies for dealing with this situation need to be planned carefully, including the use of non-contact time, classroom support, and the time required in the school development plan. At Key Stage 2, many teachers now include other age groups in the statutory testing week, either in a trial run, or in the completion of internal tests.

Records of test results should be carefully kept so that the development of a child may be demonstrated through them, especially as they spend more than one year within each class.

The structure of national testing and assessment should be recorded, and combined with any programme devised by the school. This is to ensure that there is not too much testing, and that a manageable timetable is created for the teaching staff. You need to devise a system which is easy to manage but results in meaningful assessments. These can then have a range of uses from reporting to informing the next teacher or school.

Assessment policy and its structure in Jane's school has been devised and reviewed over a number of years:

Previous experience has taught me that unless a rigorous assessment policy is in place it is very easy for continuous teacher assessment not to take place. Therefore, we have worked to achieve a policy through which we are in control and which will provide each teacher with information which can be used to assist the learning progress of individual pupils. At the same time we wanted to develop a system to record this assessment which would be on-going throughout a child's time in school, providing up-dated information related to skill acquisition and which, should it be necessary, could be used as evidence for outside agencies. The assessment policy has developed over a period of three years and is the one policy which is reviewed annually. At each review certain assessment procedures have been deleted and others added. The current policy addresses assessment issues during each term e.g. Attainment Target 1 in English is completed during October for Years 1 to 6 and on or near the fifth birthday for pupils in reception. Reviews have reduced the amount of curriculum which is assessed and the following areas are those currently in force, as shown in the example below.

Assessment timetable

Annually: at the beginning of each year children draw a whole person. This is to be stored on the inside back page of the child's portfolio: 4 to a page.

Autumn term:
October: English AT 1, Years 1 to 6
Reception children to be assessed in the term in which they start school or on their 5th birthday.
December: Technology. Link to the Christmas activity.

Spring term:
January: maths AT 1, R to Year 6
March: science AT 1, R to Year 6

Summer term:
During the first half term English AT 3, R to Year 6
April/May: reading tests
May: SATs
May/June: formal report

History and geography assessed at appropriate times during the topic. Once a year for each child. Records are kept on the assessment card.
Remaining science AT to be assessed within the topic.
Record on assessment card.
Remaining subjects on-going. Teacher assessment record on assessment cards and annual report to parents.

At the end of each academic year:
Personal self-review by each child.
Key Stage 1: choose a piece of work which they are proud of or enjoyed doing etc. Comment on it.
Key Stage 2: self-assessment of year using our standard sheet.

There are many purposes for assessment as well as meeting national requirements. These have become even more significant with the publication of results for slightly larger schools and target setting and benchmarking of a school's results against similar schools. With small schools, target setting will need to be viewed over several years to show trends, as individuals can have a disproportionate effect on the results of a small cohort of children.

It may be in the interests of small schools to keep individual progress records beginning with baseline assessment so that targets can be devised from progress over levels rather than the percentage of children attaining certain levels. In this way the target will be the percentage of children making progress, compared to the percentage who do not progress, and the levels of progress made. In this scenario the progress of children with special educational needs should be formed as a separate target based on the success of identification and what happens in the various stages of the code of practice for special needs. The use a school makes of the outcomes of national assessment is important in reviewing success and achievement within the school context.

Teacher assessment

Assessment is an integral part of the teaching and learning process enabling teachers to:

■ plan work matched to a child's or group's level of achievement;

■ identify where special help and different tasks are required; and

■ help children make progress.

It can be described under well-known headings:

Formative

This is the information the teacher collects for the next steps in learning: it informs the teaching to be undertaken. It is especially significant during the continuous programmes of work and supports the arrangements for teaching different levels within a class with different ages and abilities.

Formative assessment is a powerful tool for the teacher. Any short-term planning procedure needs to emphasise its use. It explains why the medium-term plan should not be too detailed — it could restrict the opportunities for modifying the planning at the point of delivery. Assessment also helps to inform the planning so that the pace of learning is not held back if individuals or groups make greater progress than anticipated. An exact match for every child during every lesson is not possible, but striving for a close match will produce teaching appropriate to the potential learning capacity within the group. This is particularly important when teaching a range of age groups, as the level of achievement is significant not just the age of the child.

Diagnostic

Diagnostic assessment provides a more detailed amount of information about a child's strengths and learning difficulties. It is often thought of as the standardised tests which teachers and other agencies use.

Summative

Summative assessment gives a snap shot in time of each child's achievement and is the information recorded in termly profiles, annual reports and records of achievements. They are accurate at the time they are recorded and can be reviewed later to show what progress has been made.

These methods can be identified in both Jane's and Mel's schools:

Jane:

Within the school there are two methods of recording teacher assessment. Firstly, each child has a personal portfolio book, which is an attractive foolscap-sized book, in which assessed work is stored. This travels with the child throughout the school. Secondly, each teacher has a card index file with a card for each child. Onto these cards comments about other assessed work are written plus comments about personal development or noted concerns. These cards, which can easily be used by supply teachers, have proved to be valuable at parent and teacher discussions and when writing annual reports. Their easy accessibility means they are constantly used and at the end of each year are put into the children's records. Together both records form a very realistic picture and provide sound evidence of achievement and progress.

Teacher assessment which is a part of the assessment timetable and recorded in personal portfolios has been used as a moderation exercise during staff development sessions and has enabled staff to have increased confidence when awarding annotation sheets to assessed work. It was agreed that annotation sheets would only be given when a pupil had achieved a new level. Should the pupil remain at the same level the work is placed into the portfolio with appropriate teacher comments. These comments have been useful to the next teacher when it is their turn to make judgments on assessed work.

A key issue to the success of the assessment policy has been that planning for assessment is done at the same time as the medium-term planning for the term. A standard planning sheet has been agreed and this identified the area to be assessed, the activities which will be used, the resources necessary and the objectives to be assessed. It has proved to be much easier for staff to consider assessment during the planning process than to begin to decide upon assessment opportunities when the term has begun. As with standard planning forms, copies of blank assessment sheets are kept readily available in the staff room for easy access.

Supplementary to the assessment policy is the baseline assessment procedure carried out by the teacher of reception children. This assessment which is completed during the first few weeks of a child's entry into school provides a comprehensive picture of the pupil's current abilities and is used to plan the learning process. All information gathered during this baseline assessment is stored in the record folder for the total time the child is attending the school.

A new addition to the assessment work is the evaluation of results achieved by our pupils in national tests at the end of key stages. Regular analysis of the data on achievement is enabling us to identify and support pupils who may require assistance to improve performance and also take steps to identify curriculum areas in which we may need to make alterations to delivery. This analysis is making a direct contribution to the quality of standards and is helping us to enable pupils to achieve the highest standards of which they are capable.

Mel:

In a small school with a low pupil to teacher ratio and where teachers work with children over the course of a whole key stage, there is a lot of time for individual attention and discussion. This makes the prospect of children sharing in the assessment process, in order to take more control of their own learning by setting personal goals, a real possibility. Children are encouraged to assess their own progress, evaluate their success and consider their next target. Sometimes this is the result of individual pupil and teacher conferences where issues are raised by both parties and a limited number of short-term goals are identified along with the criteria to be used to assess success. Such criteria could include reducing the number of spelling errors in final draft writing by comparing error rates over a set period of time. Sometimes progress can be demonstrated to children graphically by use of devices such as asking them to draw a picture of a Roman soldier before starting the work about the invasion of Britain, and then repeating the process at the end of the topic. The results of this activity can be shared to acknowledge the progress made by every individual child regardless of age and ability. This also supports the principles of the mission statement.

Sometimes the assessment is more formal. The key objective is to train children to recognise improvement in their work and consider what they need to focus on next to maintain their progress.

Assessment in all curriculum areas is an important part of the medium-term planning process. In order for teachers to judge whether teaching objectives have been met, assessment opportunities should be recorded in the appropriate column of the planning sheet during medium-term planning sessions. The outcomes of assessment should be used in the planning of future work and form the basis of reports to parents.

In addition to the statutory assessment programme, other assessments are carried out in the school as follows:

- before arriving in school parents are invited to help their child complete a booklet designed by the school called 'I am going to school';
- at the end of the reception year, the baseline assessment is repeated;
- further testing takes place in Year 2, Year 4 and Year 6 to track individual progress through the school;
- Year 3 to Year 5 undertake reading tests annually in the summer term.

Four forms of assessment are set out in our assessment policy.

Mel's school — Forms of assessment

Day-to-day judgments
- Teacher judgments about children's learning and progress in all subjects.
- These should inform the short-term planning process: 'On evidence I have observed the next step for this child is. . . .'
- Recording is informal (including mental notes).

Assessment of curriculum progress
- In the core areas Key Elements for assessment will be identified in policy documents.
- In all areas 'significant achievements' by individual pupils should be noted on the child's Subject Area Progress Notes (see p. 95).
- Children will be encouraged to participate in the assessment process and this involvement should be of an increasingly sophisticated nature.
- The child's Subject Area Progress Notes should be used as the basis for the annual report to parents of the child's progress.
- Work should be placed in the child's Pupil Profile Portfolio in accordance with the school's record keeping policy in order to provide evidence of progress.

Assessment of general development (social/behavioural/ emotional etc.)

■ Teachers should note any significant incidents or developments on the child's Pupil Progress Sheet (see p. 94).

■ Particular attention should be paid to events that affect the child's 'learning'.

■ These should include mention of any discussions held with parents.

End of key stage assessment

■ SAT testing in Y2 and Y6.

■ Teacher assessment made against Level Descriptions using a 'best fit approach' based on the child's current and recent work.

■ Results reported to parents as required by current DfEE assessment arrangements.

Pupil self-assessment

In line with the school teaching and learning policy, wherever possible learning objectives should be made clear to children so that they can understand the purpose of their activities, the progress they have made, and targets for future learning. A variety of assessment approaches should be developed, both formal and informal.

Other issues

■ In the implementation of the school's SEN Policy, assessment factors and achievement indicators are an integral part of the 'intervention record sheet'.

■ Assessment should be part of an on-going process.

■ A variety of techniques should be used by teachers to allow all children the opportunity to demonstrate what they know, understand or do. (Some children find it easier to express their ideas through drawing, some verbally, some with apparatus, etc.)

■ In making assessments, teachers should strive to avoid any bias according to a child's sex, race or social background.

Staff will regularly attend SATs update courses. Visiting other schools on an annual basis to compare general standards of pupil achievement is a vital element in assessing standards within a small school such as ours. All staff should become familiar with national standards in the core subjects as exemplified in the SCAA *Consistency in Teacher Assessment: Exemplification of Standards* series. Each member of staff should become familiar with the requirements at each level description in the core subjects. Examples of children's work demonstrating the school's interpretation of these levels will be built up in the school portfolio of assessed work.

Our aim was to produce a record system that was simple, quick to complete and useful. Being a very small school means it is not necessary to compile elaborate records to be passed on annually to the next class teacher, as often the next class teacher will be yourself! However, when you have the same child in your class for four years it is often difficult when you come to write their report in June to recall what an individual child did in design technology in September, for instance, or even in which year the child made a particular significant step. It was vital to establish an effective system to keep a running record to note significant pupil achievements or areas of concern. These records would form the basis of parent and teacher interviews and written reports.

Two forms were designed:
- **Pupil progress sheets:** These are for general notes including social, behavioural and emotional development and notes on meetings with parents.

- **Subject area progress notes:** These are to note significant achievements or concerns in particular subject areas perhaps based on the assessment sections of mid-term planning, and note the next steps proposed to deal with any areas of concern. The sections on this form correspond to the sections of the end of year written report to parents.

Every pupil has an individual record of work collected in a folder, which is stored in the office and updated each July. In order to make the system simple and easy to manage we decided to restrict the evidence we collect to a minimum. Data from the pupil profile portfolio could be used to assess a pupil's progress over a number of years and to demonstrate achievements or concerns to parents.

The Pupil profile portfolio must contain the following:
    English — a piece of totally independent writing, dated with the time taken noted on the document by the teacher.

Pupil Progress Sheet

Sheet no. _____

Name: _____   DoB: _____   R 1 2 3 4 5 6

Date	Technology	Concerns
Date	PE	Concerns
Date	Art	Concerns
Date	History	Concerns
Date	Geography	Concerns
Date	Music	Concerns
Date	RE	Concerns
Date	IT	Concerns

Additional comments

© **Falmer Press**

Subject Area Progress Notes

Sheet no. _____

Name: _____   DoB: _____   R 1 2 3 4 5 6

Date	English	Concerns
	Speaking and Listening Reading Writing (including spelling and handwriting)	
Date	Mathematics	Concerns
	Using and Applying Number and Algebra Shape, Space and Measures Handling Data (KS2 attainment)	
Date	Science	Concerns
	Experimental and Investigative Science Life Processes and Living Things Materials and Their Properties Physical Processes	

© Falmer Press

Maths — an example of a report or investigation.
Science — an example of a report or investigation.
They may contain the following: Photographs of achievements, any assessment results required by subject policies, pupil's own formal assessments.

The setting up of a whole school profile showing examples of standards of achievement illustrating the whole range of National Curriculum levels has been difficult to establish. Due to the limited amount of material available in a small school the whole school profile has to be built up over a number of years. We may not have an example of level 5 maths, for example, for many years. The SCAA examples of standards can be used as the basis of moderated assessment materials to support the school's own examples. It may be possible to link with other small schools to develop this profile.

Although the style and description of what has been designed within the two schools vary to reflect the different teachers and types of school, the main elements remain the same.

The purposes for assessment also can be shown to be similar for both schools: to inform planning, evaluate a child's progress and to aid reporting. The process in both schools is to make assessment on-going, which may or may not be recorded and which may also be supported by contributions from the children. These are then used to inform a profile level of assessment, which may be completed at a specific time in the year or following significant development. The purpose of this level of recording is to inform the writing of the annual formal report to parents and to provide evidence during meetings. A formal format used within one school to record the profile level of recording follows.

Systems of assessment

Both Mel and Jane have developed systems for recording and storage that match their aims for assessment, although systems are always being refined to reflect changing circumstances and to improve their overall effectiveness. Recording is most rewarding when it has a direct purpose, especially if it can be

Science profiles		
Name		
Strand of work	*Date*	*Comments*
Experimental and Investigative Science		
Life processes and living things		
Materials and their properties		
Physical processes		

used for a variety of purposes. Writing notes to inform yourself of information you all ready have will not improve the level of teaching and learning unless the intention of it is clear.

Where schools require a format to show progress over the levels for target setting, or for reporting, a simple format should be chosen which concentrates on the core subjects

Assessment levels for continuity and progression

English Strands Names	Speaking and listening						Reading						Writing					
	1	2	3	4	5	6	1	2	3	4	5	6	1	2	3	4	5	6

The Purpose of this record is to monitor the progress of the individual within a class context as they move through the school. It will be an aid for grouping and planning, as well as for setting targets for individual, group and school performance.

Recording	Year
Pen	
Red	Reception
Blue	Year 1
Black	Year 2
Green	Year 3
Yellow	Year 4
Purple	Year 5
Red	Year 6

Class Teacher

Method

At the end of each academic year mark where you have assessed the child to be currently working. For instance, if the child was working towards Level 3, the mark would appear just pre the 3 mark, as he/she would have attained Level 2.

and is completed quickly by using previous assessments. This format will still be useful for teachers who have children in their classes for many years as progress will be easily demonstrated and potential successes targeted. Again one school's approach to this type of recording is included as an example (see p. 98).

Where schools keep records of achievements for children these should be more than just a celebration of childhood, and be used for reporting current levels of achievement and for showing areas of significant progress. Some formats of record of achievements are used to store the whole range of records for the child.

Although teachers may now feel that their own assessments are not highly regarded by outside agencies it is important that they realise their significance in terms of formative assessment, which has a significant effect on the learning that takes place in the classroom. Formative assessment also gives a more complete assessment of a child than any external testing programme could. Schools should invest time in discussing the process of teacher assessment and give status to the skills teachers have in observation of children.

Formal classroom observation can provide evidence which cannot be collected in any other way. It may involve general observation as children work individually or in groups, or it can be targeted by aiming to assess a specific learning objective and may involve the use of prepared assessment sheets. It is part of existing good practice and can be the most reliable assessment available. The challenge for a teacher is in managing the class to allow formal observation to take place. Other advantages of observation for assessment is that it is successful even where there is a range of ages and abilities within the classroom and it can provide evidence for many subjects at the same time even if a specific objective has been chosen as the focus for the observation. Careful planning is needed to ensure a systematic coverage and sampling. One school has devised a model for assessment through observation to support the teachers and to ensure they feel this type of assessment is valued and useful.

A model for planning structured observational assessments

1 From your curriculum planning and knowledge of the children's abilities decide on the objectives to be assessed e.g. Programmes of Study, Statements of Attainment.

2 Is observation the only way to assess or can it be used as a check of other forms of assessment e.g. drawings, written work, discussions with children?

3 Become familiar with the task you intend to use for the assessment. Is it likely to generate the data intended?

4 Decide on the assessment criteria you intend to use for this task. Ideally try to use no more than two or three in the early stages.

5 Design the format of the recording. Ticklists with spaces for comments were used in some examples.

6 Identify the children to be observed — limit to two or three initially — and consider the effect of group members on performances.

7 From your knowledge of the children and the task consider the response that you think the children will give.

8 Decide on the arrangements for managing the rest of the class.

9 Decide if you are observing without talking; if you intend to intervene if you feel assistance is really necessary; or if you will talk with the children as well as listening.

10 How much will you involve the children in their assessment?

11 Carry out the observation and consider it in terms of practicability how informative it was, if it helped to indicate next steps in learning, if it confirmed or refuted your expectations.

12 If it was used to supplement other assessment methods it may be useful to note when there was a disparity between the two methods of assessment and the nature of that difference e.g. that a seemingly fairly able child on paper does very well in assessment through observation.

Conclusion

During the planning stage of your curriculum, highlight areas which may need some observational assessment and build it into your plans and use of time. You can also be opportunistic during any non-contact time.

The other tools regularly used by teachers for teacher assessment include:

- running records including reading comments;
- questioning and discussing;
- concept mapping;
- interviews or conferences;
- marking of recorded work;
- analysis of work compiled over a period;
- photographs and annotated work; and
- recording significant learning.

Children also play a significant part in assessments and where they are involved in their next steps for learning this empowers them to contribute to their own development. They can be involved in conferences, choosing work for records of achievement, completing prepared assessment sheets and summarising achievements.

Summary

- Have a clear manageable structure and policy which is regularly reviewed.
- Use the results of National Curriculum testing and other assessment to review and audit the curriculum.
- Maintain the high profile of teacher assessment.
- Devise a recording system that can be used for a variety of purposes.
- Review the usefulness of the assessment being made.
- Ensure that assessment informs planning, especially of continuous work.
- Consider a hierarchy of assessment where continuous assessment informs a profile level, which then informs the annual report.

Chapter 9

Schemes of work

Definition

Schools have different definitions of what a scheme of work is for so the very first task is to understand what they mean in your school. They could be defined as a mixture of the following:

- the Programmes of Study in the National Curriculum;
- a compilation of the long- and medium-term plans devised by the school;
- a compilation of all the planning in the school;
- long-term plans grouped by content rather than the terms in which they will be taught;
- long-term plans linked to subject guidance for the class teacher; and
- the organisation of the Programmes of Study and National schemes of work to create the school's own syllabus.

There are two broad types: those compiled from actual work and plans within the school; and those which lead the planning for the teacher. The first type is where schools work out what effective teaching means for particular age groups, based on experience and knowledge of the National Curriculum, and then link their plans to the Programmes of Study. Any gaps are then addressed perhaps by programmes being allocated to a specific class or time in the year, especially for blocked areas of the curriculum.

Each book in *The Subject Leader's Handbook Series* has a section on schemes of work.

The second type is typically used by commercially published schemes, which can dictate the content and pace of teaching within a class or the learning programme for particular children. Some curriculum areas may be delegated by the subject leader to each class or age group to create a coherent programme of work. This tends to be more common with subjects which are traditionally taught independently from the general class topic but may be linked to the topic as long as it is not too contrived or compromises the subject's overall progression. The increasing number of national schemes of work provided to schools may mean that a small school's main task is adapting these to suit the needs of the individual school.

Jane:

Work on writing the schemes of work is in the early stages of development in our school. Following our OFSTED inspection, a key issue was to continue the development of schemes of work, which would support the delivery of the curriculum. Whilst it is acknowledged that an agreed comprehensive scheme provides a solid structure on which to base teaching, experience of writing schemes of work with a small teaching staff is that they are very time consuming to write and demand much personal commitment by the staff. However, not daunted, and with an action plan to fulfil, the writing of the necessary schemes was identified over a 5-year timescale in the development plan. Immediately, by being realistic about time and personnel restrictions, pressure was lifted and worthwhile discussions began about which scheme would be the most practical one with which to start.

The results of the discussions were that the current commercial maths and English schemes, which were being used throughout school, had previously had gaps identified and remedied and staff familiarity with them was seen as an advantage. End of key stage performance indicated that teaching pupils using these schemes was producing good results. Whilst no commercial scheme was completely followed for science, the structure of the long-term plan employed by the school gave clear guidance for the delivery of the Programmes of Study and the various commercial material extended teacher knowledge.

The next step was to list in priority those subjects for which there was no structure in place and to choose one for which the need for support was greatest. It was agreed that the delivery of the music curriculum would benefit from specific guidance.

Mel had to devise schemes of work to deal with the large age range within each class and again found the different subjects should be managed differently. In the content area of science, for example, a scheme was devised which created three phases for the children to experience, whilst the continuous programmes were devised to allow for group or individual progression. The process chosen can also be seen, as well as highlighting the process for very small cohorts of children:

Our schemes of work represent the mobilisation of current policy. Schemes of work detailing curriculum content and learning outcomes were developed through the medium-term planning sessions over a number of years. The detailed medium-term planning sheets built up to form detailed documentation of tasks, outcomes, approaches, expectations, progression, continuity, resources and assessment opportunities for all subjects and all age groups.

For example, in the teaching of every area of science, referring directly to National Curriculum statements, we made decisions about the content to be covered throughout the whole school. This had been divided into three stages of progression for Key Stage 1, Years 3 and 4, and Years 5 and 6. In this way we feel assured that each aspect of science will be visited three times by every pupil with tasks being set which ensure the continuity of approach and progress in the degree of challenge offered to pupils. The learning objectives identified in the medium-term plans and tried and tested in the classroom were then formalised into schemes of work.

We are dealing with year groups of less than 10 children; occasionally a year may only contain one child. With such small pupil numbers schemes can be modified to become individual programmes of work. Schemes, therefore, have to be broad and flexible, outlining intended progress from Reception to Year 6. Each child, or group of children, can then be placed in the appropriate place on that continuum.

Use of commercial schemes

Schools using commercial schemes often admit to it apologetically, but when used carefully they can contribute very successfully to a child's learning. This is especially true when they are not in control of the teacher–learner relationship, but rather complement the aims of the teacher to increase the knowledge and skill of the children. Schemes should be checked as to their coverage of the Programmes of Study and the opportunities to foster the learning process. One way, for example, is to use the scheme for maths within the school and then use a variety of commercial material to facilitate it. This means that the pace of learning is set by the teacher and there will be less of a rush just to complete a book and allow children to move on to higher order work before they have assimilated the present level. Groups can be organised to be introduced to a subject, which they then will work on at different levels. This is the method used in the Literacy Hour, although in classes with many age groups different texts may be required to cope with different maturity levels. If used without care commercial schemes can demand a very rapid turn over of content with little time for reflection, communication and different levels of tasks.

Mel discusses the use of commercial schemes in his very small school:

> Published schemes are used selectively to support our learning objectives. In all areas of the curriculum we have tried to draw upon a wide range of published materials.
>
> For example, having produced a set of learning objectives for each age group in maths, materials were bought to implement these ideas. A published maths scheme based on learning through practical experience, which breaks the teaching of maths into small steps and came with comprehensive teachers' file, full advice and extension activities, is used as a core scheme throughout the school. It is not intended that we should follow the scheme rigidly but use it as a central core of materials, which can be supplemented by the teacher's own ideas, and materials from other sources.
>
> A similar approach was used in the area of handwriting and spelling with the purchase of a published scheme that supported our intention of combining spelling and handwriting. The resources are geared towards individual development and can be used in an on-going capacity throughout the school.

Rather than stick to one reading scheme a collection of reading books from a variety of publishers have been organised in a progression of levels to facilitate a structured reading programme in which the children have choice within a given range of books.

Producing schemes of work

Developing a format for recording the schemes of work needs certain levels of flexibility to take changing class organisations into account. Blocked work especially can create problems if class arrangements are changed in any way. As discussed earlier in the section on long-term planning, it is important not to let blocked work dominate school planning.

You will need to decide whether advice should be included for teachers within a scheme of work. The problem is that the documents can become so long that they are difficult to use, particularly as every teacher will have so much information when dealing with the full range of subjects. You may find it useful to develop guide booklets for a range of difficult subject areas rather than produce complete texts which may contain excellent guidance but are never read. Examples of documents which could be developed are, for example, information on materials in science, getting the best out of artefacts, using calculators, spread sheets on a computer, children researching for information, teaching fractions and so on. The advantage of this system is that the documents can be made available for staff meetings and preparation reading will be simplified. It is also a system which can be adapted to include new information without the need to re-publish the whole set of materials. Initiatives such as the Literacy Hour can then be dealt with as a supplement to the established published materials. Teachers who attend in-service, can also easily share their new knowledge in staff meetings by producing guideline documents.

Jane describes the development of the scheme of work for music in her school and the format for recording the decisions:

It was established that the scheme would follow the same format as the long-term scheme in that it would cover the work for Key Stage 1, Years 3 and 4 and Years 5 and 6. However, it would not be broken down into terms as it is in the long-term planning. Each programme would be addressed separately. Throughout the construction of this scheme the knowledge of the subject leader was invaluable, but the overall work was the result of contributions from all staff using their expertise and experience.

The resources that contributed to writing the scheme of work were:
- long-term planning;
- medium-term planning sheets;
- short-term records of work for activity ideas;
- commercial materials used in the school;
- radio, television etc.;
- materials obtained at training courses;
- peripatetic staff;
- outside agencies working in school; and
- taking an audit of the musical resources.

Whenever possible, if there could be a common theme, subjects were linked — such as the links between sound in music and science, or period music linking music to the Tudor study. Ideas immediately started to flow and we continued matching music to the long-term planning, but ensured it was not contrived. The National Curriculum documents were referred to throughout and this helped increase familiarity with the Programmes of Study and gave the subject leader opportunities to explain those areas where there was misunderstanding or confusion.

The final product addressed the following areas:
- title — identifying curriculum links;
- Programmes of Study;
- learning objectives;
- activities; and
- resources.

To date, work on the scheme is still continuing as the refining is taking place e.g. further activities are added with supplementary ideas. The process is time consuming but the completed product does ensure that pupils benefit from the precise progression of skills and at the same time there is enormous staff satisfaction from working together to produce a working document.

As Jane has shown, there is no prescribed format for a scheme of work. It could vary between a grid and a list based on the long-term plans. The introduction of a structure to develop skills for children further advances the aims of the long-term plans. In a small school a skills progression could allow for a blocked base of work to be presented to a range of children who will be expected to work on it at different levels. When studying a history study unit, for example, some children may be reacting to a picture source whilst others are comparing information from various sources and others are commenting on the reliability of the sources. In this way children could develop through a scheme of content at an appropriate level, with opportunities to develop higher order skills when using different historical content.

A skill structure can be devised from the Programmes of Study and Level Descriptions of the National Curriculum, and there are also worked materials published which could be used as a starting point. This type of work is usefully developed when small schools come together for in-service or allow subject leaders to devise a basic progression which is then adapted by each school.

One of the most notable aspects of the case study schools is that the schemes of work always seem to be under review and are rarely described as being completed, even if the work on them is finished for that period. This reflects the schools' desire to retain some flexibility and to keep up to date with National Curriculum developments. It might seem a little frustrating never to feel the work has been finally finished but this is overcome to some extent if the work is sectioned, time restrained, and completed for that period.

Managing national strategies

Adapting and implementing national strategies, which are generally designed for single age groups within each class, can appear daunting for the small school and headteacher with a class to teach. The school should first consider where their strengths already lie within the subject and make that the basis for their response, while at the same time identifying any areas which may cause concern.

The National Literacy Strategy, for example, can be viewed as a useful tool to ensure effective coverage of much of the

Positive aspects of mixed age teaching

- Differentiated task setting comes naturally to the teacher of a whole key stage class as it takes place every lesson already.
- Children in mixed age classes are usually already trained in independent work.
- Children are already trained to work in mixed age groups.
- Teachers are aware of individual children's differentiated needs from several years of contact with the child.
- It is easier to make use of technology, such as listening centres and computers, as small schools tend to have greater access to these facilities.
- Older children can act as role models and enhance the learning of younger children.

English curriculum. It is important to distinguish between its content and delivery. The structure of the Literacy Hour is not that far removed from the structure of most well-organised lessons, having an introduction, middle and conclusion, carried out with pace, rigour and clear objectives. In most teaching and learning policies all of this will already be included. In a small school class the suggested timings of the hour may have to be restructured to allow a 'ripple approach' to the lesson organisation where the teacher shares text with perhaps two age groups of children while the others work independently and then the groups interchange. This may include other subjects so that the hour actually takes ninety minutes, but is an hour long for each child. When seeking to adapt a strategy essentially written for single year group teaching it is important not to lose sight of the positive elements of mixed age teaching and exploit these advantages within each lesson.

Within the small school, continuity is enhanced as there are fewer teachers to train and training activities will be more often experienced at first hand for each staff member. Any changes and modifications may be quickly initiated, as there are fewer staff to liaise with. There does, however, have to be a degree of flexibility, which keeps to the spirit of the Literacy Hour, including its structures, but which allows for the creativity of the teacher to respond to the children in the class because of the fluctuation numbers in a year group, the spread of ability and the range of maturity. These factors may change the focus and emphasis and delivery within each academic year.

Strategies for planning remain largely the same as for other subjects, with the 'macro to micro' system of long-, medium- and short-term planning.

It will be advisable to phase in any national strategy so that the first step is to allocate the time and devise a teaching timetable and then:

- Feel your way in by trying out ideas during the initial implementation period and then evaluate them with the staff.
- Decide which areas are best matched to individual children, which can be delivered to single or double age groups, and

which to the whole class e.g. objectives for Year 4 delivered to a whole Key Stage 2 class.

■ Develop subject knowledge amongst the staff.

In smaller primary schools it is possible to devise a continuous development pathway for children in each literacy area, such as in report writing. Some work may be even approached as a whole school project to encourage excitement and help children recognise the stages of development they pass through. Plays and playwriting, for example, could be a used as a learning pathway, with every child able to contribute at their own level, generating whole school enthusiasm and commitment.

Some work can be delivered to a whole key stage, but with restrictions placed on different groups. An example is a discussion on summary writing, followed by some children writing a summary of a historical event using writing frames to support the work, whilst other children use either a single text or a range of different texts. This also allows the use of existing books in the school and contributes to a range of other subjects. During numeracy work, the use of investigative and open problems allows for a spread of ability, so children can work at different levels of understanding. Information technology can also be used within national strategies, with the added incentive of widening the experiences of children in small schools by use of the Internet.

Summary

■ Decide on the definition of a scheme of work for your school.
■ Use work that has already been completed, such as the long and medium plans.
■ Decide how guidance material is to be published.
■ Plan the use of any commercial schemes to increase their effectiveness.
■ Formats will vary according to the school's definition and by subject.
■ Set the production of schemes into a manageable time scale.
■ Phase in national strategies, starting from work that is already established.

Chapter 10

Policies

Producing policies

School policies are a record of the thinking within a school; the formal publication of how the school ethos affects each curriculum area. They are often produced as a result of in-school discussion and training, using expertise within the school, supported by information from advice and in-service training. Guidance can be gained from documents such as the National Curriculum inspection handbook and may be based on a format devised by the LEA.

The production and review of policies takes considerable time and clear thinking, especially as they represent the distilling of opinion from the whole group involved in curriculum management. A typical model in slightly larger schools is for preparation to be undertaken by the subject leader who brings a draft policy based on an agreed format to the teaching staff; the staff then discuss and make suggestions; and finally the curriculum committee of the governors review the policy and recommend it to the full governing body. Very small schools may increase their efficiency by producing joint policies.

A policy review is most successful if a prepared set of questions is devised, given to those involved to prepare and then opened up to general discussion at the review meeting. Following this the subject leader views the recorded opinions, matches them to the current policy, and then makes proposed changes if necessary. In very small schools changes may be recorded directly onto the policy during the review meeting.

Policy format

The format of each policy should be consistent so that it allows quick assimilation of content and facilitates delegation. A consistent format will ensure a policy document emerges based on agreed criteria. Each subject policy could contain the whole range of issues from assessment and special needs to resources; or there could be a core policy of teaching and learning to which each subject policy document refers. In this latter model the specific policies would include any information about teaching and learning which is individual to that subject. Mel developed a standard format in his school:

> Attempting to formulate policy documents at the end of the school day along with other pressing issues is not the ideal climate to produce meaningful statements of policy, so we employed two supply teachers to release both members of staff to consider and record policy statements.
>
> Recording policies directly onto the computer saved the secretary's time and meant a draft could be printed out at the end of the day for staff members to consider immediately and suggest amendments for the final copy. We use a set format, which we found speeded up the process and created a uniform format, making them easy to read and understand. Our ideas were:
> - introduction;
> - aims;
> - entitlement;
> - the nature of that subject;
> - implementation;
> - health and safety considerations;
> - assessment and recording; and
> - resources and review.

Jane also concluded that a standard format for all documents should be adopted and describes how every staff member was involved in the initial production. She also includes a list she uses to remind herself of the management of the writing of policy documents by the subject leaders:

The knowledge that they had to start writing policies led to much discussion about which area to start with and what format should be followed. Concerns were expressed about the length of each policy, where it would be stored, and who would read it once it had been written. After we had begun the task what emerged was that the process was perhaps the most useful aspect of policy writing. Throughout the process of writing individual policies whole school procedures were reviewed and updated often leading us to make alterations to systems at the same time. Staff who were unfamiliar with specific structures had valuable opportunities to gain information.

In reaching a decision about which format to follow we sought advice from a variety of sources and some standard policies issued by the LEA, for example, a budget management policy could be used as a starting point. However, what failed was trying to adapt a policy belonging to another school to suit our school. After one attempt at doing this it was agreed it would be quicker to write our own which was specific to us. Our format for most policies is:

- mission statement;
- aims;
- objectives;
- content;
- cross-curriculum issues;
- learning and teaching styles;
- equal opportunities and special needs;
- resources;
- homework; and
- assessment.

Whole staff agreement must be reached before a policy is considered finalised and the process of writing has been spread over the period identified in the development plan. It is difficult to write one policy after another so by identifying processes for writing and reviewing in the development plan it ensured they were written at regular intervals in an on-going process which is not repetitive.

As policy writing is time consuming and an onerous task for staff it was important to spread the load over time allowing them to be both a leader and group member.

The following list of guidelines can be used to manage the process as the writing takes place:

- Is there a fair spread of work among staff?
- Are staff involved in other major work e.g. Key Stage 2 SATs?

Each book in *The Subject Leader's Handbook Series* has a section on developing policies.

- Be realistic about individual subject leaders. Some will need deadline dates for sections to be brought to the staff for discussions.
- Discuss as you go.
- Encourage staff to understand that draft copies are for discussion and alteration.
- Always go through the final draft together to check agreement.
- Include a review date.
- Be realistic about length as long policies are less useful.
- Thank the subject policy leader and praise successes.
- Store policies in the files.
- Be realistic about the production each year.
- Take the final draft to the governors for approval.

Summary

- Organise the process and timescale for policy production.
- Use a standard format for each policy and decide on storage.
- Develop a timetable for review.
- Devise a process for the review.
- Store on disk to speed alterations.
- Use the work of others as starting points so that time is effectively used.

Part four

Monitoring the curriculum

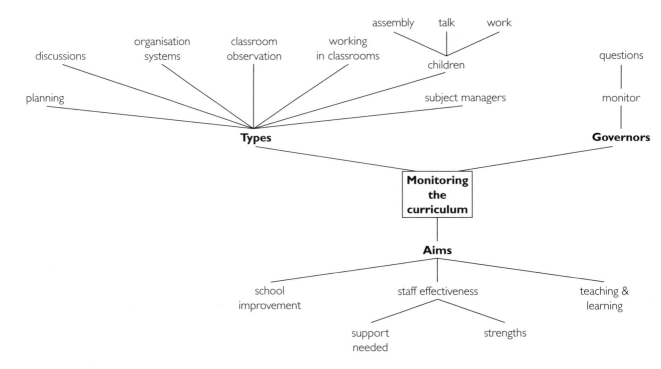

discussions

organisation
systems

classroom
observation

working
in classrooms

assembly   talk   work

children

subject managers

planning

questions

monitor

Types

Governors

**Monitoring
the
curriculum**

Aims

school
improvement

staff effectiveness

teaching &
learning

support
needed

strengths

Chapter 11

Monitoring the curriculum

All those with an involvement in managing the curriculum in a school are also involved in its monitoring and evaluation. Teachers, governors and external agencies all have various levels of involvement in this process. The local education authority will increasingly use the target setting and assessment statistics to monitor school performance, so small schools need to be clear about how the monitoring systems are set up and used within the school. Monitoring and evaluation by governors and teachers will be considered here.

Governors' responsibilities

Governors are responsible for ensuring that the legal requirements of curriculum delivery exist in the school. As they cannot be involved in day-to-day issues a level of monitoring needs establishing so that they can take an overall view and monitor and evaluate the decisions they have made which affect the curriculum. Examples might include budgetary allowances for employing new staff to support larger class size, the effectiveness of large purchases such as a new reading scheme or restructuring areas of the school. They can achieve this level of monitoring and evaluation in a variety of ways:

■ Spending time in school with a specific focus, such as children's response to a new reading scheme or how a newly formed library is being used.

- Asking appropriate and previously agreed questions to relevant personnel e.g. are there enough new books? How have parents responded in the home book? Is the library organisation system manageable for children?

This type of monitoring means the governors can hold informed discussions and feel the statutory obligations are being met. It can also avoid the difficulties experienced when non-professional visitors enter professionals' classes, so encouraging shared dialogue. Governors, heads and staff should agree a code of practice for visits with some training provided for the governors as a feature of developing their skills as monitors.

When monitoring and evaluation is taking place, it is best to restrict the range to be viewed as it is impossible to cover everything in one short visit or observation. Schools and external agencies are gradually developing tools to assist the process; for example, benchmarking provides statistics which can be used to evaluate the curriculum in the context of knowing the actual details of the school. Additionally, a school's own portfolio of assessed work, and nationally provided expected learning outcomes for the curriculum subjects, provide a standard against which an evaluation of the success of the school curriculum can be measured. An informed monitor and evaluator will be able to use information generated in this way to reflect on the potential outcomes within the school.

Types of monitoring

Monitoring by teachers and even the headteacher is difficult in a small school because their is often a very small amount of non-contact time. This may be alleviated by the creation of different layers of monitoring. A very detailed level will need a budget requirement, such as a supply teacher, to facilitate classroom observation. Aspects of literacy and numeracy are obvious targets for this detailed level of monitoring. The next level involves whole staff participation in monitoring the development plan, OFSTED action plan or school policies and schemes of work, even if this is only a discussion about the progress made. This second level also includes the use of the school's portfolio of collected work. A timetable has been devised by Mel to ensure this is carried out and spreads the demands over the years of the development plan, as shown in the Year 3/4 policy review reproduced below.

Year 3 — Policy review timetable

	Term 1	Term 2	Term 3
Attitudes and values	Teaching and learning Quality and expectations	Assessment and Record keeping	School aims Self-esteem
Curriculum	Art/Writing	Maths	IT
Planning			
Admin. policies	Behaviour/Bullying Severe weather	Fire	

Year 4

	Term 1	Term 2	Term 3
Attitudes and values	Teaching and learning Quality and expectations	Pastoral/Marking	School aims Equal opportunities
Curriculum	Speaking and Listening RE	History	IT
Planning		Long-term planning	
Admin. policies	Behaviour/Bullying Severe weather	Health and Safety Fire	

A lighter level of monitoring consists of analysing work on a regular basis, perhaps as one item on a staff meeting agenda. The lightest level of all is the answering of agreed questions, especially those devised for governors and linked to the development plan.

One of the most effective types of monitoring is when teachers spend time in another class observing or teaching to evaluate effects of curriculum development and monitor the stage of development. In this way the aims of the exercise to help each other to do the job more effectively are clearly visible.

Analysing the quality of teaching and learning

The overall aim for monitoring and evaluation is to reach opinions about the effects of developments on the quality of teaching and learning within each classroom as well as the general level of quality within the school.

Other aims are:
- to improve day to day happenings in school;
- to offer staff opportunities to evaluate the effectiveness of their own teaching;
- to determine the different support individual teachers may require; and
- to establish the particular contribution each member of staff might make to raise teaching standards as a whole.

A school's self-evaluation needs to take an objective view of pupil achievement and underachievement, so that they can determine the strengths and weaknesses of the teaching and learning within the school. It is an opportunity to establish whether the school's stated aims and intentions are being met and provide information for the school's development plan.

Evaluation and school improvement enables us to:
- monitor performance;
- analyse achievement throughout the school in comparison with other schools;
- evaluate the quality of teaching and learning and the social and moral development of the children;
- plan in order to enhance the school's achievements by setting clear goals; and
- act on the information provided to improve the quality of all aspects of school life.

Mel describes the process of monitoring and evaluation for his school:

Regular and continuous monitoring of all aspects of school life forms the basis of our school development planning. It is important to match our monitoring of success and weaknesses to our school aims and ethos, it would be a mistake to concentrate solely on one area such as academic test scores. Above all we try to remember to:

> measure what we value
> rather than
> value that which can be easily measured.

In our very small school, where year bands have included as few as one pupil, the statistics of SAT scores, even when considered over time, are a poor indicator of standards attained or progress made. Test scores, therefore, tend to indicate individual pupil attainment and development rather than whole school performance, especially if figures are expressed in percentage form.

In this light we will be using test performance, benchmarking and value added indicators as a tool to help us monitor individual achievement. It is more appropriate for us to set individual pupil targets and involve the pupil in the process through discussion.

Using primary school performance indicators clearly identifies which children are performing outside the expected achievement in comparison to pupils of similar age across the country. Children with particular weaknesses are identified and appropriate action is taken. The information provided by testing is used to challenge individual pupils. Used regularly throughout their time in school, each pupil's rate of individual progress can be plotted.

When seeking indicators of attitude, behaviour and personal development we ask: Do children demonstrate:
- Interest in their work?
- Sustained concentration?
- Expected standards of behaviour in and around school?
- Politeness, trustworthiness and a respect for property?
- The ability to develop constructive relationships with other children and adults?
- Respect for other's backgrounds, feelings, values and beliefs?
- Good attendance?
- Punctuality?
- Initiative?
- Willingness to take responsibility?

Whenever standards require further improvement, or if they seem to be slipping, ways to remedy the situation are discussed, put into action and evaluated. The discussion includes all relevant parties to the situation to help create a positive solution. Action may be swift and immediate, such as an assembly focus, or may require detailed long-term planning and budgeting. Our evaluation establishes whether the solutions have had an effect and may also involve pupils.

Although Jane has a large teaching commitment she has devised a list of the ways in which she personally monitors and evaluates the work within the school:

- discussing with staff their term plans and half term reviews;
- organisation of timetables;
- classroom observation;
- working in classes;
- talking to children;
- examining children's books;
- discussions with curriculum leaders;
- mentoring new personnel;
- general staff discussions;
- overseeing weekly forecasts;
- curriculum reviews; and
- monitoring resources and their use.

In order to make monitoring and evaluating a process which benefits the development of individuals and the school, a focus is agreed at the beginning of each term e.g. the development of spelling throughout school, and all visits etc. are based upon this focus. It helps attention to be brought to areas of the curriculum which are under-addressed, poorly resourced and highlights pupils with particular abilities.

Following visits to classes teachers are invited to discuss the observation with the headteacher and a brief record of the visit is kept and this is most useful when evidence on the focus is collected at the end of the term (see below). Further professional development which emerges from the findings can be identified within the personal development section of the school development plan.

Monitoring and evaluation

Class:
Teacher:
Observer/participator:
Date:
Purpose of visit:
Points raised at discussion:
Targets — if appropriate:

Subject leaders who monitor in classes are asked to discuss their findings with the headteacher before meeting with individual members of staff.

Governors also have an important role to play in monitoring and evaluation. Every half term a governor is nominated to spend time in classes. The role is not just as an observer but to participate as much as possible. All governors, even those with initial reservations, have expressed their enjoyment of their time in school and agreed it opens their eyes as to what happens in the classroom. The governing body now have a much clearer understanding of day to day school life and pupils are now familiar with governors. As with staff who observe in classes, governors also agree an area of focus for each half term and report back at full meetings. Often this will be based on a specific interest — special needs or equal opportunities. It is part of the process that the governor discusses their observation with the headteacher first so that explanations can be prepared.

Just like the list prepared by Jane to describe the monitoring and evaluation she uses, another school produced a list for subject leaders. The purpose was to reassure them that even if regular classroom observation was not possible, the process was still on-going. It was an opportunity for them to verbalise how they carry out their duties in this area, as part of their job description, as shown in the example below.

Monitoring the curriculum

The methods currently in place include:
- school work portfolios;
- staff meetings where our planning is presented to each other;
- 'Show and Say' assembly, which also occasionally features a particular aspect or subject of the curriculum;
- open classrooms where work is on display;
- informal conversations;
- staff meetings for each subject;
- policy reviews as shown in the Development Plan;
- Programme of Study review and allocation within each key stage; and
- feedback opportunities following courses.

We aim to develop this to include opportunities for subject managers to work in other classrooms. This can be in a variety of ways:
- observation;
- working together on a piece of work;
- teaching while the teacher observes.

Each book in *The Subject Leader's Handbook Series* has a section about monitoring.

Subject managers should also have opportunities for non-contact time to review resources, research, reading etc. but we acknowledge the restraints of funding. Some non-contact time may be provided by imaginative use of time which has no cost.

Summary

- Monitor developments of the school development plan.
- Use statistics as a guide to individual achievement alongside school effectiveness.
- Prepare monitor duties along with targets.
- All staff and governors have a role in the process.
- Evaluate success of developments, policies and curriculum delivery using prepared benchmarks and school knowledge to set a context.
- Analyse the range of monitoring already being used.

Part five Resources

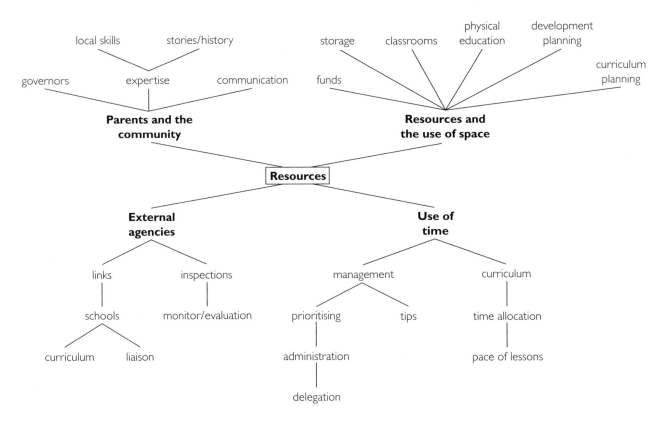

Chapter 12

Resources and the use of space

The planning of resources provision is part of the curriculum and management audit which results in a costed three-year development plan. Decisions should be made about who has responsibility for spending by considering various models:

■ will all funding be held centrally;

■ will funding be delegated to each class teacher; or

■ will funding be delegated to subject leaders.

Whatever model you choose, make sure that funding is not diluted into too many small areas which will purchase nothing of significance, or where money may be spent on items which are not of the highest priority but are chosen for being affordable. As well as aiming for some flexibility to take advantage of unexpected opportunities, it is desirable to link spending to the development plan and to provide the regular consumable resources. It may be good practice to have a signed agreement with governors to allow for immediate spending of the portion of the budget for which they have responsibility in case opportunities for resources arise unexpectedly. For example, when the LEA find money to support information technology.

The purchase of resources is most effective when it is combined with planning of the curriculum. More focused spending can be budgeted once a curriculum becomes established. For example, books can be bought for the library for the topics that have been planned, as well as materials to

Each book in *The Subject Leader's Handbook Series* has a section on resources.

broaden knowledge and information. When teachers have devised long- and medium-term plans, they will have a very clear idea about which resources they require, further helping to focus spending. These resources will then be well used; thus offering good value compared to equipment bought on a whim which never leaves the storeroom.

Smaller primary schools have smaller budgets so some items are proportionally more expensive purchases. An office computer, for example, will cost the same for any size of school. It can also be difficult to provide a variety of resources, for example, a range of construction toys, for the same reason. However, remember that every purchase of a major item will provide a resource for a larger proportion of the school population. Any support funding from other sources also resources a greater proportion of children compared to the same amount for a larger school.

Some equipment will be consumable and so will need regular reviewing and replacement. Technology equipment and some tools, some science equipment and even scissors, for example, may be designated as consumable items and purchased annually. Teaching is difficult without enough consumable materials even if expensive items are well resourced. To ensure consumables are always in stock a model could be:

- subject leaders for technology, science and art annually purchase consumable material;
- class teachers are delegated funds for class consumables so they can focus spending on the year's programme;
- class teachers are delegated funds to provide equipment needed for the delivery of long- and medium-term plans; and
- major items of equipment are purchased with full staff agreement according to the development plan.

Good management of resources may require subject leaders or class teachers to have some designated non-contact or in-service time to release their potential. When planning to introduce new information technology hardware, for example, a programme of funding should be complemented by a programme of staff development.

All sizes of schools have many creative ideas for fund raising to enhance the resources in the school. When seeking support for these events, parents and others are likely to be more supportive if they are also aware of the aims of the fund raising and how the resources purchased fit into the wider management of the school and the curriculum.

Once resources are in school they should be stored in a way that makes them easy to retrieve if they are effectively used. Some types of storage may need to be costed into the initial purchase price and the storage thought out in the initial stages of planning resource provision. An example could be the purchase of storage boxes for construction toys, or extra shelving. It may even be in a school's interest to consider improving the storage of present resources before new ones are purchased.

Jane explains resources provision in school:

One of our aims is to:

'ensure by sensible financial management that the educational environment and resources which the children use are of the highest possible standard.'

Resourcing to a continuous standard of quality is expensive and has called for whole staff agreements on the use, sharing and storage of resources by adults and children. Subsequently, decisions on the purchase and use of resources are more specific and must fit that purpose for which they are needed.

Linked to the school development plan are subjects for curriculum development, from one of these staff reach a decision on which will be a priority. This area will have substantial extra funding in comparison to other subjects. Not all the funding is spent at one time and each teacher can offer suggestions and ideas. It has proved to contribute to staff keeping up to date with latest resources.

Subject leaders have as part of their responsibilities the monitoring of the quality of equipment related to their subjects. At the start of each financial year they are requested to submit curriculum bids for equipment. Through experience I have found that if you delegate money to subject leaders without their having access to discussion, equipment may be purchased only for it to be found that it already exists in another classroom. Introducing a bidding system has led to expensive resources being re-cycled releasing money for other areas.

Headings on a bid form might include:

Subject area:

Development area:

Financial year:

Resources:

Cost–item–price:

The effective purchase and use of resources is linked to the long-term planning. Once a planning cycle is in place resources can be acquired which are used for the particular topic. Topic boxes are organised with an inventory attached to the back of the subject policy. The use of equipment lists, re-organisation of resources and demonstrations of new equipment are ideal staff development ideas for late summer term when staff are feeling weary of policies, schemes etc.

Sometimes another avenue is explored which will have an impact on raising curriculum awareness and providing resources at the same time. As in many schools a 'Book Week', with a variety of events, also included providing books for the school library.

Use of space

In very small schools some resources may have to be centralised in one teaching area and either passed between classes or made available to children when required. A lack of space is not one which can be entirely solved by spending or applying for capital resources beyond the control of the school, but is one which needs to be resolved by thoughtful management and cooperation. This can mean organising the use of space in a different way, and reviewing regularly the use of rooms including exchanging rooms to enable larger classes to be taught in larger rooms. All areas, even if they are very small, should be reviewed so that the potential for use is maximised.

Internal reorganisation may involve small amounts of capital expenditure, which could be from the delegated budget where possible, or be a fund-raising target. In these cases a school should check whether the LEA would contribute towards costs, perhaps on a 50 per cent basis. Presenting ideas in the context of a development plan may prove the most effective method. It is also very worthwhile investing time in building up relationships with the team that are responsible for school repairs.

As with other subjects, the physical education programmes may be restricted by a shortage of space, especially if there is no hall, or there is only a small outdoor area. In these situations, a school would be advised to concentrate on areas that can be taught well within the limited space, and to work on other areas occasionally. For example, some small schools join with other schools for days of athletics or team games using secondary schools' facilities.

Space in Jane's school is a difficulty, which she describes as being 'an accepted issue', and they have tried to minimise its effects:

Recently the school has undergone some modernisation and using and improving an old back cloakroom has provided a separate headteacher's office. This now provides a space for private interviews with parents. Previously the staffroom was the only venue for this. This created some problems although these were limited by making specific times available for interviews of which everyone, including parents, were aware.

The design of the playground, which contains listed outside toilets which are no longer used, creates problems for the delivery of the physical education curriculum. The school has no hall; therefore, certain aspects of physical education such as gymnastics cannot be done. Having spent much time taking advice and trying to resolve this problem I have come to accept that alterations have to be made to the curriculum and that we address in greater detail and time other areas e.g. team games etc. Using the local village hall has also been tried but the pupils received more exercise walking to and from the hall in all weathers than time spent in it, especially as it does not have appropriate equipment.

As furniture has to be moved for assembly etc. some very expensive tables which collapse safely and securely were purchased, with support from the parent-teachers association. This furniture when collapsed moves easily on wheels allowing the whole school to gather, albeit crowded, and pupils can make presentations in front of their peers.

School concerts and performances which are a major feature of the music curriculum are held in the village hall and problems with winter weather and transporting children is resolved by booking transport with a small charge to each family. Without doubt, a sight never to be forgotten was to see an entire school walking from school to hall during glorious summer weather dressed in 1960's hippie clothes!

During the past two years the use of space has been accepted as an issue. What was once a television area, which was used infrequently throughout the week, is now a most attractive reception area for the school secretary. By moving the television to a classroom and making simple readjustments to timetables, the school now has the facility of a waiting area, space for the secretary and most importantly an area where visitors can report without walking directly into classes.

Some very small schools have severe space problems and these can dominate the whole school ethos if allowed to. The management of the curriculum may need to take space into account but cannot afford to become dictated to to such an extent that the statutory requirements of the curriculum are neglected. The experiences described by Mel show that active management can resolve the problems of multi-use rooms, lack of a hall, no classroom sinks and little storage space. Once an attitude to resolve problems begins it can open the creative ideas of everyone through lateral and positive thinking.

Very small schools have an advantage over larger schools in that they do not have to buy large quantities of equipment to ensure all the children have equal access. One set of the latest construction kit may be shared by five or six children in a year band, a school with a two-class intake would need to purchase 10 times this amount to provide the same ratio. Children in small schools often have well-developed computer skills due to more opportunities for hands-on experience. Our school currently has a ratio of one computer to eight children, a ratio unlikely to be matched by many larger schools.

Once the initial purchase of equipment has been made, we ensure that it is well looked after and available to every child. There is little waste. In small schools responsibility is truly collective with no one person assigned to tidy areas so everybody is involved and everybody cares — children and teachers.

The main draw back in a small school, however, is that when you have purchased the equipment there is no space to store it. Storage and space in general tends to be scarce in small schools, which are frequently Victorian in construction. There is usually no running water or sink in the classroom and lunch is often eaten in the classroom or, as in our school, the whole school gathers in one room to eat lunch together.

Rooms must be multi-purpose environments with desks being pushed aside to create space for assembly or Key Stage 1 physical education lessons. The Key Stage 2 room converts to a dining room by the application of tablecloths, which are then folded and stored by the children after the meal while a shift system of monitors sweep the floor. The staffroom is also a television room, special needs area, story-telling room, library etc. Procedures have to be designed for carrying dirty painting materials to the cloakroom sinks in a blue plastic box, to be returned clean in a red plastic one and replaced on their appropriate storage shelves.

Furniture must be chosen that is easy to move and can serve a variety of functions. All equipment must be accessed easily and children trained to return items to their correct place. This may require purchasing additional storage or making alterations to existing furniture, but is a major factor in achieving independent learning and effective use of space.

Time spent sorting, storing and labelling equipment boxes is rewarded by smooth lesson organisation, quicker clearing up and the creation of extra space. We have painted strong cardboard delivery boxes, great fun for the children, for a cheaper and effective way of storing difficult items such as cardboard tubes, plastic pots and fabric. The challenge is to keep the school neat and tidy to make maximum use of its space but at the same time ensure things are readily available and easy to access.

The need to try curriculum resources becomes apparent during the medium-term planning sessions. Order sheets are kept at hand during the planning meeting and items required for the next term's programmes of work are noted as we go along. This links our spending directly to the curriculum needs and spreads the cost of developing curriculum resources over a period of time. Specific items of stock identified during long-term planning for the year, such as videos, are ordered during the summer term for the following academic year.

In the absence of a school hall our Key Stage 1 children use the classroom for indoor activities while Key Stage 2 children walk to the village hall during the autumn term to spend an afternoon a week on floor work in gymnastics, dance, country dancing and drama activities. It is our vigorous games programme at Key Stage 2 that compensates for the lack of gymnastic facilities, along with outdoor climbing equipment purchased through the support of the friends of the school and a sports council grant, to enable children to climb etc.

Being a very small school it was possible to take all children swimming during one term each year by taking a summer session not used by a local secondary school. This generates annual enthusiasm for swimming and a determination to improve on last year's performance. It has ensured children learn to swim at an early age and over the course of their time in primary school one term a year equates to the same time as children swimming every term in Years 5 and 6.

Human resources are another vital source of curriculum expertise and support. The local vicar visits school readily to take assembly and is available to help in religious education lessons. Other expert visitors include local historians, representatives of various religions, students, music teachers and parents.

Finally, it is worth contacting your LEA on an annual basis to request help in providing space for the delivery of the curriculum. Often this is more effective if the requests are from the governors who can formally ask for replies to their requests so they can inform governors during full governing body meetings. Even if this is not successful, keeping records of your appeals will be useful information to give to school inspectors to show you are actively seeking to resolve accommodation difficulties.

Summary

- Resources requirements should be noted, costed and ordered during long- and medium-term planning sessions.
- Purchase of consumable items should be linked to the planning.
- Major items of equipment should be budgeted for as part of the school development plan.

- Storage needs to be planned.
- Some equipment purchase will require a linked in-service programme to ensure effective use.
- Space problems should be resolved if they cannot be solved.

Chapter 13

Use of time

Effective use of curriculum time

Making the most of available curriculum time can be
thought of as the long-term allocation of time to individual
subjects, and the pace individual lessons are organised.
When devising a time allocation for subjects over the year the
process can be simplified by acknowledging at the outset that
the timing will not be precise for every week due to unforeseen
circumstances and a changing pattern of curriculum delivery
over the year. Encourage staff to produce general time
guidelines which can be used for calculating weekly time
allocations for each subject. This exercise needs to be
continually under review as new initiatives are introduced,
such as the Literacy Hour. Time guides create a system which
is useful for teachers when designing the balance of the
curriculum.

Start by finding out what current time allocations are for each
subject and then adjust them as necessary to ensure delivery of
a broad and balanced curriculum.

The pace of lessons can be monitored when a teacher is
observed such as during appraisal, inspection, mentor
observation and general monitoring by the school's own staff.
This can provide useful information which can be fed back
into reviews of the management of the curriculum. In addition,
external inspectors will comment on whether a lesson was

pacy in terms of overall organisation, efficient explanation, tasks relevant to the different levels and the expectations of work completion and standards achieved by the children.

Curriculum management can influence the pace of lessons by:

- providing easily retrieved resources;
- encouraging a model of lessons which reviews previous work, has a relevant exposition by the teacher, has tasks which are matched to the learning requirements of the children, has a plenary session;
- developing planning formats which emphasise specific objectives for learning;
- developing a purposeful ethos where punctuality and careful preparation complements the cooperative work of both staff and children; and
- introducing short pacy skill practice at the start of some lessons, such as maths.

The effective use of curriculum time has been organised at Jane's school:

Effective curriculum management is dependent on knowing what is being delivered in the classroom. The best method of being in control of this area is to have guidelines on subject time allocation and timetables which directly relate to these.

Planning of the actual time taught was based on a 36-week school year. Key Stage staff discussed the variance between the stages as curriculum demands differ and the resulting decisions of time allocation are used to plan the weekly timetable. In order to be realistic everything which happens in school was calculated, including the amount of time spent travelling to the swimming pool! This led to discovering that an incredible proportion of time was spent on the bus and an immediate review of swimming took place. As an exercise, calculating curriculum time spent on each subject is very interesting and often leads to expressions of surprise about the amount of time which *should* be spent, and how much is *actually* spent. The following is an example of a format for recording, which we used:

Time allocation at Key Stage 2

Week: 23 hours 45 minutes
Year: week × 36 = 855 hours, excluding collective Worship, lunch and breaks.

Subject	Recommended time	Actual time (in hours)
English	162 + 18 (in other areas)	252
Maths	126	153
Science	72	81
Music	45	45
PE	45	63
Art	45	36
History	45	45
Geography	45	45
DT	45	36
RE	45	45
Hymn practice		18
French		18
PSE		18
IT		18
(and through other subjects)		
Totals	693	855

Individual schools will have their own curriculum priorities depending on different factors. By analysing actual curriculum time spent on each subject, opportunities are provided to alter the allocation as demands arise, such as when introducing the literacy and numeracy strategies. Having actual calculations ensures that subjects are not under-taught and greatly supports teachers in planning weekly timetables, ensuring that a broad and balanced curriculum is implemented as statutory requirements demand. Organising the amount and use of non-contact time in a small school also needs careful planning.

Time management

Many headteachers focus on time management during their appraisal and cite it as the most difficult aspect of their work as they try to maintain the quality of their teaching with all other aspects of the role. The importance of time management in a small school is to allow you and your staff to be able to concentrate on teaching, and to prevent management time becoming taken over by administrative chores. You could try:

- delegating administration to your secretary as much as possible;
- investing in training for your secretary;
- using an answer phone requesting callers to leave a message, send a fax or try ringing again later;
- creating organised, colour-coded filing systems with a guide to the contents; and
- dealing with issues immediately.

Mel acknowledges the difficulties and shows how time can be used effectively by being well organised, flexible in approach and realistic in expectations of what can be done:

The day passes like a roller coaster ride. There seem to be a hundred and one things to put into action, remember or make a decision on, and on top of that you have a class to teach and have playground and other duties. Such is the everyday life of the headteacher of a small school. Time must be cherished, defended and never wasted. I quickly discovered that to survive as a teaching head you have to be thoroughly organised and have a carefully prepared filing system. A place for everything and everything in its place is particularly pertinent for the small school where time and usually space are at a premium.

Developing speed reading skills was essential in order to assess the mail which arrives daily. The correspondence is organised into piles of: action required, pass to the secretary, file until later and throw into the rubbish bin (most falls into the latter category). I do this during coffee break each morning. An efficient filing system is vital. If there is a place for everything it can confidently be stored until needed. Catalogues and product information is stored in subject sections, different agencies, inspection, etc. are all given their own file. Items not filed immediately tend to hang around for weeks so it pays to be organised.

It is impossible to remember all the ideas that pop into your head as you go about the business of the day. A set of note sheets on a notice board with titles including:
- remember to order these
- don't forget to mention to the adviser and
- when the building inspector calls . . .

and so on, is a real help. Once your idea is safely written down you can continue with the day without worrying about forgetting it.

> Keeping a notebook handy to record all those jobs that you need to do is also a very reassuring idea. It keeps you informed of tasks to be completed, gives you a sense of satisfaction when you cross jobs off the list once you have done them and proves, by way of the many jobs that remain, that they were not as important as first thought.

All sizes of schools feel there is never enough time to do everything they would like to achieve. Staff in smaller schools will have this same feeling, but it is often intensified if they have to work on every curriculum area across a range of ages. Jane has many tried-and-tested tips to contribute:

- Plan the next annual calendar of events — performances, sports day, parent meetings etc. — before you break up at the end of the academic year.
- At the same time, record in the diary the dates that letters will go home to parents informing them of the events.
- At the start of each term remind parents of forthcoming dates.
- Set the date for sending home annual reports to parents and the final date for submission of the reports to the headteacher.
- Plan realistic programmes of staff development.
- Ensure staff who have a major role in forthcoming curriculum development know well in advance so they have time to prepare.
- Set starting and finishing times for all meetings and keep to them.
- Circulate meeting agendas in advance and take minutes.
- Make bookings for external trainers as soon as possible.
- Arrange courses as soon as possible and book supply teachers as soon as confirmation of attendance is received, writing all details immediately in the diary.
- Use a dated concertina file, read the post and delegate the mail to the appropriate date space. This ensures important documents are safe and are dealt with in the relevant time.
- Establish that curriculum medium-term planning has to be submitted by staff no later than two weeks after the start of term.
- On the first day of each term set dates with individual staff to discuss planning etc.
- On the first day of term set up monitoring and evaluation dates.
- Set appraisal dates well in advance.
- Have a large whiteboard in the staff room and keep an up-to-date two-week programme displayed.

- Set realistic targets and review their progress.
- Keep master copies of forms, planning sheets etc. together near the photocopier which is readily accessible to everyone.
- Keep staff informed — do not spring surprises.
- Remember the greatest cause of stress is a lack of information!

Summary

- Early, and thorough, planning helps use time effectively.
- Devise systems of planning and administration which are efficient for your school situation.
- Allocate times for all subjects.
- Encourage staff to keep their lessons pacy.

Chapter 14   External agencies

The range of groups who have an interest in your school is remarkable. The list of people who have regular contact soon grows, and it is the responsibility of the school to develop effective relationships which combine to enhance the quality of teaching and learning. These 'insiders' include: parents, governors, purchased service employees and so on. Parents and governors require open communication and enjoy being welcomed into the school.

'External agencies' are those which the school voluntarily contacts and those with the statutory duty to become involved with the school. Voluntary contacts may include liaison groups, linked schools, visiting speakers, students, local business links and so on, and can be used to provide first hand experiences for the children and to develop subject knowledge. The advantage to a small school is to broaden the range of adults children have contact with and to extend the range of experiences the staff can refer to. Time needs to be organised carefully so the links provide positive developments and do not become a burden. There are other agencies who visit the school to carry out statutory inspection, monitoring and evaluation.

Mel describes the voluntary groups with whom his school is attached:

One of the great challenges for village schools is to overcome the isolation which comes from working in a small self-contained unit, often in a remote location. A network may be a possible answer to share expertise, develop policies, organise in-service training, form headteacher support groups etc. However, in a world of market forces the notion of supporting groups of schools can be difficult to arrange. Often, in our area, groups are formed consisting of schools who have a common link other than geographical location including size, religious affiliation or similar challenges.

Our school is involved in three main groups: a religious education group of local church schools, a physical education group of small schools and a primary–secondary liaison group of partner schools. There is also a larger group of small schools, less than 80 pupils, from the whole county who meet to share ideas and form a united body to present needs of small schools to the LEA.

The religious education forum meet to share ideas, organise in-service and develop resources. An example was the purchase of sets of Judaism artefacts which were boxed and stored in the larger schools providing more resources without storage problems for the smaller schools. The group also works closely with the local diocese education office and advisory teacher who provide funding support, contacts, expertise, advice and knowledge.

To overcome the obvious difficulties for a very small school in fielding competitive teams a group of small schools joined to provide opportunities for children to enjoy friendly tournaments. This allowed every child to represent the school at some point in their school career without having to compete against large local primary schools.

Our primary–secondary group meet readily to discuss current issues, arrange cross-phase teacher exchange visits, monitor the progress of children in Year 7 and organise joint events. One of the most popular events organised is the annual music evening in which all partner schools combine to form a huge choir and perform in the sports hall of the secondary school. Other events organised for Year 6 children at the secondary school include sport activity days and part days.

The support of local advisory teams has allowed us to call upon the expertise of subject specialist advisers, enlist the services of an artist in residence, use the support of the special needs department and take advantage of curriculum resources like the mobile computer unit.

The school library provides topic packs of non-fiction material and a mobile library which visits each term.

There is, of course, the usual access to departments such as the behaviour support unit, physically impaired agencies, the educational welfare officials, buildings division etc. Representatives from the police, fire department, etc. are regular visitors supporting themes such as: People Who Help Us.

Inspections

When the school is going to be monitored, evaluated or inspected by external agencies your aim should be to prepare before the event, monitor during the event and prepare for the period following. Start by raising the teachers' awareness of what will happen and why it will happen. If you have requested monitoring by the LEA advisory staff, everyone should be aware of the reasons for the request and what will be happening. Statutory inspection requires much awareness-raising. Use the book produced for OFSTED preparation, experience within the school and any other experience which can be called upon.

Long-term planning should take inspection into account so the teachers feel they will be in control of the curriculum during the inspection period. Early preparation of mid-term plans will facilitate support, resources, and an opportunity to present evidence across the widest possible range of curriculum subjects.

Monitor your staff during inspection so that you can support your staff appropriately. Don't hesitate to inform the inspectors if a particular individual is being strongly affected by the process. It is also a function of this monitoring to provide extra materials and evidence to support judgments especially of issues that seem to be emerging. This can be in the form of photographs, extra documents, children's work etc.

You should prepare carefully for the post-inspection period. You will need to be prepared to produce an action plan and inform parents and governors; and you will need to be ready to

For a full discussion of OFSTED inspections, see *The Primary coordinator and OFSTED re-inspection* in this series.

minimise the impact that follows even a positive inspection. One idea is to give opportunities for the staff to release tension through whole staff discussion, organising a breathing space, and encouraging informal discussions to flourish. A format to contribute to this is to meet for a brief recording of ideas under the following headings:

Inspection wisdom	
Things that went well to retain:	Things I would do differently next time:

These completed sheets can then be shared, explained and stored for future reference.

In Jane's school the inspection process created feelings with which many schools will empathise:

What better excuse is there to implement reviews for the curriculum, policy, planning procedure etc. than the arrival of the letter from OFSTED bearing news of the inspection? Thoughts of school education and the desire to receive a good report will ensure that everyone begins to focus seriously on what happens in school.

When our letter arrived, the school development plan was reviewed in detail to identify what could be realistically completed and to make sure procedures the inspectors would want to see, but we could not possibly achieve, e.g. schemes of work, were clearly identified within the development plan. This proved satisfactory to the inspection team.

Some worthwhile tips learned during the process are to take the short-term planning very seriously and set dates for the medium-term plan to be completed in advance so that necessary alterations can be made and criteria such as differentiation is satisfactorily covered. Offer staff adequate time to organise the display throughout the school ensuring that a cross-section of the curriculum is on view. During staff development sessions we talked through the information required from subject leaders and during the inspection week the leaders were pleased that this had been prepared as it enabled them to provide evidence and to control nerves.

Almost two years after the inspection the action plan is still influencing curriculum development. We were asked to consider the use of firsthand resources and this has led to a review of procedures for educational visits. Whilst visits were always related to topic work it is now common policy for adults accompanying the visit to have a review with the teacher who prepared them for the visit.

Preparation involves the learning objectives with main teaching points highlighted and an explanation of terms. Adults assisting with visits have expressed appreciation of this as children not in the teacher's group still have their attention drawn to the same objectives and received explanations based on the teacher's notes. This has been a good development for our school and has raised the value and the quality of educational visits.

Summary

- Don't become isolated.
- Take part in joint ventures with other schools.
- Join primary–secondary liaison groups.
- Take advantage of local education support.
- Seek out community links.
- Visits for inspection, monitoring and evaluation should be well prepared.
- The post-inspection period should be carefully thought through.
- Action plans should consist of short-term issues and long-term developments.

Chapter 15   Parents and the community

Communication is vital

Communication is probably the key management skill in a school's relationship with parents and the community. For the purposes of this book the community is defined as the local groups and individuals who have contact with the school. Church schools have the contact through their foundation with the local church, although many county small village schools also have close ties with the local church.

There are many types of communication a school can have with parents. These include contact with the class teacher for information on their child's progress, and general information about the school, the curriculum and for fund raising. A programme of formal meetings regarding children's progress can be linked to a more informal invitation to visit the school (although this may need to be reviewed if security locks are necessary).

Communication regarding the curriculum needs some planning as there are always new families connected with the school. One solution is to hold an information meeting for new families each year where background information can be related over general subjects including the management of the school, planning, assessment, special needs and communication systems. A meeting with all reception parents should concentrate on reading, daily contact systems, organisation issues and an introduction to the Key Stage 1 curriculum. The other meetings a school may wish to organise during the year will then concentrate on new curriculum developments. One idea to consider is whether the first meeting of the school year between the class teacher and parents will be more beneficial if it is an open meeting for all parents who receive an explanation of the curriculum for the year. This works well in the small school situation and can replace repetitive individual meetings, which try in a very short space of time to explain the curriculum.

Mel explains the communication used in his school:

We send newsletters to parents every two or three weeks. They provide a venue to announce forthcoming events, publish children's writing, request help for resources, and inform people of current developments in the curriculum. Newsletters also go to regular supporters of the school. We have a mailing list of 56 with only about 21 families in the school and a copy is placed on every village noticeboard. These are a vital part of keeping the school alive in the community and is the main form of communication between the school and the outside world. The older village inhabitants make a special point of telling us how much they enjoy reading the newsletters and how important it is for the community that the school is so active in this way.

Parent–teacher interview evenings are held once a term to inform parents of the child's progress and they also receive a written report at the end of each academic year. The interview provides the opportunity for parents to:
- look at the children's books and displays;
- discuss the child's general achievements;
- discuss areas of future development for their child;
- seek clarity about the curriculum and school policy;
- raise any general concerns about the child's progress; and
- communicate any issues from home affecting progress.

The interview provides the opportunity for the teacher to:
- communicate their professional assessment of the child's progress;
- clarify the significance of SAT scores;
- raise issues of academic or behavioural concerns;
- clarify school policy;
- suggest ways in which parents can support their child;
- gain a valuable insight into the child's background; and
- establish home–school contact.

Other opportunities for parent–school dialogue are created on the basis of individual need including:

- the presentation of awards;
- reports in the newsletter;
- informal contact when children are collected;
- telephone calls;
- notes in the reading book or home book;
- an appointment to meet after school; and
- reviews as part of the code of practice for special needs.

A curriculum evening for parents is organised each year on a subject which parents suggest through communication in the regular newsletters. These evenings provide an opportunity for us to show parents what is going on in school, to broadcast its ideas, to explain the thinking and processes behind education decision making and to demonstrate the professionalism of its staff. We attempt to make these evenings entertaining, amusing, fast paced and with audience participation. Hopefully, parents and interested members of the community experience an entertaining evening and feel more informed and confident of the methods and ethos of the school. Popular subjects for such evenings have included information technology (we used the county mobile unit to provide extra hardware), reading, number and writing.

Jane also has a structure of meetings to keep parents informed, including the two elements of general curriculum awareness-raising and information regarding children's progress. Systems evolve over time and are continually reviewed to check effectiveness and purpose.

Curriculum awareness-raising for parents begins before their child starts school. An important part of the induction process for new parents is the curriculum evening when parents of potential reception pupils spend an evening in the reception class, which is set up as it would be for a normal day, and have the learning objectives of the various areas explained to them in terms of the Desirable Learning Outcomes for under-5-year-old children. Explanations are supplemented by photographs of pupils working in the areas and lists of the skill being acquired are situated prominently beside each area. This has proved to be an ideal opportunity for the class teacher to reinforce the reason for play and how it is an integral part of the Desirable Learning Outcomes.

During the same session the reception teacher and headteacher will talk about the maths, English and reading schemes which are in place. Parents are free to ask questions. Perhaps the greatest effect of introducing parents to the idea of curriculum evenings early on in the child's school life is that the parents see curriculum evenings as an important part of school–parent liaison and are eager to attend the termly subject evening for parents, staff and governors.

The appeal of the termly curriculum evenings did not happen easily and the first organised curriculum evening was cancelled through lack of support. When reflecting on this I realised that to have cancelled was a mistake and that the success of these events would only happen once parents had began to attend and talked about them to others. This was exactly what did happen and now the attendance rate is high. A good idea was to encourage Year 5 and 6 pupils to attend and to bring a parent with them. We began with a subject people feel confident with, including the curriculum leader. Governors who attend these curriculum evenings show a greater understanding of the school's curriculum aims, are more understanding of the teachers, are realistic in expectations of curriculum development and will discuss documents with increased confidence. This is an important element as curriculum involvement is now seen as a necessary part of the role of the governor.

Parents of Year 6 pupils have during their final year a meeting each term which is regarded as an important part of the preparation of Year 6 parents and pupils for secondary education. One of the meetings is attended by the lower school heads of the transfer secondary schools. Each lower school head is given individual space and parents have an opportunity to talk to them about any matter about which they require information.

At these meetings the teacher of Year 6 and the headteacher will talk to parents about the Year 6 curriculum and the expectations of achievement e.g. levels of attainment through teacher assessment and national tests. Parents use this information as part of the process for making informed decisions about the future education of the child.

Two years ago a system of informal monthly consultations was introduced. This after-school session takes place on the first Wednesday of each month and both adults and children can attend. There is no appointment system and parents may speak to the teacher if they wish but usually they are content to look at the work in books and on display. Parents enjoy these opportunities to talk with their child about the work and at the same time they are absorbing information about the curriculum.

Twice a year more formal parent–teacher consultations are held which follow an appointment system. No children are permitted to attend so explanation can be more appropriate to adults. Even if parents do not take advantage of every opportunity they know it is in place and this appears to reassure them.

Extending opportunities in the community

The wider local community can be a good way to enrich the curriculum, broadening the opportunities for children in areas of curriculum knowledge and also contributing to their personal and social development. This is especially significant for children attending a small school. Local industry or businesses may offer expertise, information or resources. Local individuals may have stories or resources that are useful. When studying the local history and geography, for example, local contributions can make the study more relevant, and can provide a different viewpoint which will make the children review their own response to the local environment. Schools can make a contribution to the community in return, not only through the education of children, but by direct actions such as caring for a patch of land, or entertaining local groups. The list below shows the contacts developed by one school.

Community links

Governors
A parent community committee exists, one of their tasks being the production of a newsletter.
The school also has links with the church confirmed by its Voluntary Controlled status, including a weekly assembly taken by the vicar, church services and an annual competition to design the Christmas edition of the parish magazine.
Parents are encouraged to be in school, including providing classroom support.

Parent–Teacher Association
Exists to provide a communication link and for fund raising.
A range of activities are organised each year including:
    Two village coffee mornings (Village Hall)
    Rummage Sale
    School Fair, including a social event (e.g. Picnic Disco)
    Quiz (Sheets on general sale at many local outlets)
    Book Fairs

School Supporting the Community
1   We have a village project, maintaining a local amenity area which we helped to create (Fir Tree Corner).
2   Class 4 children produce a 'radio' programme for the local History Society to be stored in local archives.
3   Free lettings for the Brownies and Guides.
4   Charged lettings (e.g. History Society).
5   Administrative facilities used free of charge by the playschool group (e.g. photocopying).
6   Use of the Village Hall (charged) e.g. annual concerts, coffee mornings, which are supported by the general local community as well as parents.

Supporting Charities
1   Paying for a child's education in India.
2   Whale adoption.
3   Bi-annual sponsored event.
4   One-off activities (e.g. Children in Need).
5   Local Church Fund through the annual Christingle Service and Harvest Festival.

Community Supporting the School
1   Annual art competition.
2   Free paper and card from local firms.
3   Regular on-going village fund raising activities (e.g. Quiz nights).
4   Occasional appeals for specific targets such as the building refurbishment project e.g. Round Table, local businesses.
5   Curricular support provided by local contacts e.g. History Society.
6   School events advertised in local establishments.

Mel and Jane described some of the contacts made by their schools:

Jane

Recent participation in a sewing exhibition, in which all 90 children joined, lead to intense local interest and assisted the continued development of curriculum relationships. Many older residents are eager to be a part of our school life, and enjoy working with children and have valuable skills to pass on. Similarly they are eager to talk to pupils about their experiences of, for example, the Second World War or what the school was like when they attended it. A recent tape made by two very elderly former pupils has held a captive audience for quite some time and the children never tire of hearing their tales.

Mel

A warm invitation to school events is always extended to all members of the community. Regular school events include productions, barbecue, autumn fair, disco and quiz nights. The school is often used as the place for police surgeries and visits from the fire department. Children take part in the events organised by the village committee and held in the village hall such as musical celebrations and the village show. The village church plays a big part in the community and we support it by holding harvest, Christmas and Easter services there along with a special end of year service for the children about to leave for secondary school.

Summary

- Communication is the key to parent and community links.
- Plan a system of curriculum meetings, which are open to governors too.
- Be aware of the needs of new parents.
- Use local contacts to enrich the curriculum.
- Encourage children to contribute to the local community.

Index